LEADERSHIP
STRATEGY
AND TACTICS

ALSO BY JOCKO WILLINK

Discipline Equals Freedom

WITH LEIF BABIN

Extreme Ownership
The Dichotomy of Leadership

CHILDREN'S BOOKS

Way of the Warrior Kid
Marc's Mission
Where There's a Will . . .
Mikey and the Dragons

LEADERSHIP STRATEGY AND TACTICS

[FIELD MANUAL]

JOCKO WILLINK

MACMILLAN

First published 2020 by St. Martin's Press

First published in the UK 2020 by Macmillan
an imprint of Pan Macmillan
The Smithson, 6 Briset Street, London, EC1M 5NR
Associated companies throughout the world
www.panmacmillan.com

ISBN 978-1-5290-3297-0

1 3 5 7 9 8 6 4 2

A CIP catalogue record for this book is available from the British Library.

Designed by Steven Seighman

Printed and bound by CPI Group (UK) Ltd, Croydon, CR0 4YY

Visit **www.panmacmillan.com** to read more about all our books
and to buy them. You will also find features, author interviews and
news of any author events, and you can sign up for e-newsletters
so that you're always first to hear about our new releases.

THIS BOOK IS DEDICATED TO THE MEN OF

SEAL TEAM THREE, TASK UNIT BRUISER,

WHO TAUGHT ME HOW TO LEAD,

ESPECIALLY:

MARC LEE, WHO TAUGHT ME THE VALUE OF LIFE.

MIKEY MONSOOR, WHO TAUGHT ME THE MEANING OF SACRIFICE.

RYAN JOB, WHO TAUGHT ME TRUE PERSEVERANCE.

CHRIS KYLE, WHO TAUGHT ME ABOUT DEVOTION TO DUTY.

AND SETH STONE, MY BROTHER, WHO TAUGHT ME ABOUT
LOYALTY AND FRIENDSHIP, AND NEVER LET ME DOWN. EVER.

CONTENTS

LEADERSHIP STRATEGY AND TACTICS

INTRODUCTION

THE ROOTS OF LEARNING LEADERSHIP

When I reported to SEAL Team One after completing Basic Underwater Demolition / SEAL Training (BUD/S), there was no leadership course. New SEALs were issued no books or materials of any kind on the subject. We were expected to learn to lead the way SEALs had learned for our entire existence—through OJT, or on-the-job training.

Of course, there are some advantages to OJT. It is helpful to be coached and mentored by a solid leader who trains you as you go through the real challenges of your actual job. In the SEAL Teams, that means a leader telling you exactly what to do in various scenarios as you go through them. If your leader happens to be a good leader, is willing to invest in you, and if you are smart enough to pay attention, you will eventually learn something about leadership.

But there are some major shortfalls to this method of teaching leadership. First of all, not all leaders are good leaders, and the SEAL Teams are no exception. When I got into the SEAL Teams, it was

1991. There was no war going on. The first Gulf War had just been fought, but the ground war was over in just seventy-two hours. SEALs only conducted a small number of operations, and they were relatively easy. Almost all other deployments before that, for the better part of twenty years, had been peacetime deployments. SEALs' primary task had been training other countries' militaries. Actually engaging in combat seemed a far-off dream to me and to most of us in the military. The reality was, the SEAL Teams—and the rest of the U.S. military—had been in a peacetime mode since the end of the Vietnam War. That meant leaders weren't really tested. A great leader in the SEAL Teams got pretty much the same assignments and advanced just as quickly as a bad leader.

There was no guarantee that the leader in a platoon who was supposed to be mentoring young SEALs was the type of leader who should be emulated. On top of that, not all leaders are looking to mentor their subordinates. Furthermore, even the best leaders can only truly invest their time and knowledge in a handful of their people. Even during peacetime, there is a ton of administrative work to be done, and there is a good chance that leadership coaching and mentorship will slide off the schedule.

For the junior SEALs, it was incumbent upon them to pay attention. But there were also plenty of distractions. Sometimes it was difficult for a junior member of the team to understand he would not always be a new guy—that one day he would be a leader in a SEAL platoon, and he needed to learn everything he could so he would be ready.

I was lucky. I had some truly great leaders who invested in me. They took the time to explain things to me. They talked me through strategies and tactics. Some of the Vietnam SEALs told stories that held important tactical leadership lessons. I listened. Those stories and lessons sank in. Eventually, I was able to put the leadership theories I had learned to the ultimate test—in combat. I then codified those lessons and passed them to the young SEALs entering the ranks. I tried to teach them how to lead.

The goal of leadership seems simple: to get people to do what they need to do to support the mission and the team. But the practice of leadership is different for everyone. There are nuances to leadership that everyone has to uncover for themselves. Leaders are different. Followers are different. Peers are different. Everyone has their own individual characteristics, personalities, and perspectives. I often tell leaders that what makes leadership so hard is dealing with people, and people are crazy. And the craziest person a leader has to deal with is themselves. That being said, even crazy has a pattern; there are patterns to human behavior. If you can recognize the patterns, you can predict the way things are likely to unfold and influence them.

When I retired from the military, I started teaching civilian leaders the same principles of combat leadership. Eventually, I partnered with my former SEAL teammate Leif Babin and started a leadership consultancy called Echelon Front. The principles from the battlefield applied to any leadership situation. We wrote about the tenets we had learned in combat in two books about our experience as combat leaders and how the principles of combat leadership apply to business and life. The books, *Extreme Ownership* and *The Dichotomy of Leadership,* explain the principles in clear language and showcase the principles in stories from combat and the business world. The feedback from leaders around the world has been incredibly powerful as they apply the principles from the books to their worlds.

But applying the principles can be more challenging than it might seem. While garnering an understanding of the concepts is fairly simple, sometimes it takes more. A leader must understand the strategies and tactics needed to actually implement these principles—how to pragmatically put the principles to work. He or she must understand the strategic foundations on which the principles are built and the core tenets that comprise those principles. Then the leader must understand the tactical skills, strategic maneuvers, and communication techniques used to employ the principles of leadership. That is what this book is about.

Like other books I've written, the experiences I describe are based on my memory, which isn't perfect; the quotes are not verbatim, but approximations meant to convey the ideas that were spoken. Some details have been altered to protect the identities of the people involved or sensitive information.

This book does not need to be read only sequentially from cover to cover. It is written and organized to be used as a reference so that any leader can quickly understand and implement the strategies and tactics relevant to the situation he or she is facing. *Leadership Strat-*

egy and Tactics is meant as a field companion to help leaders do what they are supposed to do: *lead.*

Who am I to try to teach leaders how to lead? Where did I learn leadership? Much of my leadership education was luck. I say it was *luck* because there were a few fortunate coincidences that gave me the right frame of mind, the right teachers, and the right opportunities to learn.

One of the ways I was lucky and that made me focus on leadership was the fact that I wasn't really that naturally talented at anything in particular. As a little kid, I wasn't the fastest or strongest or smartest. I was never great at shooting a basketball, kicking a soccer ball, or throwing a baseball. I didn't win any races or have a shelf of trophies and ribbons from sports. My report card was never exceptional either. I might have done well in a class if I was interested, but I usually wasn't, and my grades reflected that. I was average across the board.

Still, at the core of my personality, I wanted to do well. I wanted to leave an impression on people. I wanted to leave a mark, but my athletic and cognitive skills didn't always allow it. So even from a young age, I needed to get others with more talent and more skill to do what I needed them to do. I needed to lead.

Of course, I didn't think of it as leadership. I just thought I was making things happen and contributing by getting people to work together, to support one another, as we moved toward a common mission. Maybe that mission was building a fort in the woods or planning a mock military assault with squirt guns on another group of friends. Whatever the task was, I generally found myself giving direction to people who were stronger, faster, or otherwise more capable than I was. That seemed to be where I could help the most and the one area in which I could perform with a higher level of competency.

I've also always had a rebellious streak. Maybe it was another way for me to leave a mark; I wouldn't conform to the way other kids acted. I acted differently, listened to hardcore and heavy metal music, and had a hardcore attitude about things. That attitude set me apart from the pack. Once on the outside of the "normal" kids, I was detached from them. So I observed. Looking in from the outside, I garnered a better understanding of the people I was watching. I saw their emotions, their cliques, and their drama unfold from a detached position. I learned.

My rebelliousness reached its pinnacle when I decided to join the navy. Many of the other kids in my small New England town were smoking pot, drinking, and listening to hippie music. After high school, many were heading away to college or going into a trade. Joining the military was one of the most radical things a kid from my town could do. I took it one step further: I tried for the SEAL Teams.

In the late '80s and early '90s, no one knew very much about the SEAL Teams. My navy recruiter had one bad copy of the SEAL recruiting video entitled *Be Someone Special*. While completely cheesy by today's standards, at the time it provided me with a window into the SEAL Teams: machine guns, snipers, explosives, and high-speed operations. It was like a dream come true. I enlisted.

When I told my father I was joining the navy, he told me, "You are going to hate it."

"Why?" I asked him.

"Because you don't like authority, and you don't like people telling you what to do."

"But, Dad," I responded confidently, "this is the SEAL *Teams*. It is a team. We don't take orders. We work together."

What a naïve kid I was. Actually, I was just plain stupid. I thought the SEAL Teams were just groups of guys who worked together, flat organizations where no one was really in charge. Not even close. I also had heard that the SEAL Teams had a 50 percent casualty rate and that almost no one made it to a twenty-year retirement because most SEALs were wounded or killed. Mind you, this was 1989, but other than the invasion of Panama, where combat operations lasted only about a month and a half, we weren't at war. Looking back, I'm sure this idea of a 50 percent casualty rate was rooted in the fact that the predecessors to the SEAL Teams—the Naval Combat Demolition Units, or NCDUs—had suffered a 50 percent casualty rate during the D-day invasion of Normandy Beach. I didn't know that at the time. I thought all SEALs had a 50 percent casualty rate, and I believed it. It made me even more eager to be a part of the SEAL Teams. Like I said, I was dumb. Tough, but dumb.

But joining the navy was still the best thing I could have done. It gave me a blank slate and clear direction. No one in the navy cared that I didn't have the best grades in high school. It didn't matter that I wasn't the best athlete. No one was concerned about where I was from, what my parents did, or about anything else in my history. They shaved my head, gave me a uniform, and told me what I needed to do to be successful. Make your bed like this, fold your underwear like that, polish your boondockers until they look like mirrors. If you could follow the rules and do what you were told to do, you would be put into a leadership position. I did follow the rules, and I did what I was told to do, and it paid off. I was made a squad leader in boot camp. What does that mean? Technically, not much at all, but it meant a lot to me. I was successful. But more important, I had found a home.

BUD/S was the same way for me. I still wasn't great at any particular skill. Not the best runner or swimmer. Not great at the obstacle course. But I could do what I was told. I could play the game. And I wasn't going to quit. Some people say that everyone thinks about quitting during BUD/S. I never did. Not for a second. The thought never crossed my mind. Hell Week, a five-day block of continuous physical training with almost no sleep whatsoever and which causes the highest number of people to quit, was actually relaxing for me, because during Hell Week, nothing is timed. During all other facets of BUD/S, students are constantly on the clock. Timed runs, swims, and obstacle course evolutions take place every day. If you miss the time and fail one of them, you are "on the bubble." If you fail again, you are out. It was stressful. But during Hell Week, nothing was timed. You just had to keep going. You just had to not quit. For me, that was the easy part.

When I got done with BUD/S, I checked into SEAL Team One. I

was fired up, as all of us were who were checking into that sacred place of war heroes and legends. We were proud we had graduated BUD/S and were ready for life as SEALs. There was one problem. We weren't SEALs yet. And we had no reason to be proud, as we soon found out.

The master chief of the command, the highest-ranking enlisted SEAL at Team One, welcomed us aboard. "No one here cares that you made it through BUD/S. We all did. It doesn't mean anything here. You have to prove yourselves to earn your trident. So keep your mouths shut, your ears open, don't forget anything, and be on time. Any questions?" The trident was the gold insignia worn on the uniform, which indicates you are a SEAL. To receive our tridents, we had to go through a six-month probationary period and then go through a written and oral review board with the senior enlisted personnel at the team. We were all nervous about that, and the master chief provided no comfort whatsoever.

None of us had any questions for the master chief. That was a humbling moment. Despite having been through BUD/S training, and despite being told that the training was "elite" and "special," we realized very quickly that we weren't. The rest of the new guys and I still had a lot to prove, and somehow, I knew I always would. That is one of the underlying themes of SEAL Team culture: you can never rest on what you have achieved in the past. You always have to improve.

In the early '90s, when I got to SEAL Team One, the training progression was different from how it is now. Back then, once on board a team, you were eventually assigned to a SEAL platoon. This is where you would actually learn to be a SEAL. Up until that point, the training wasn't tactical. In BUD/S, you don't learn very much at all about the actual job of being a SEAL. You learn how to be cold, wet, tired, and miserable and not to complain about any of it. But you don't learn any of the job skills that make you into a professional operator. Those skills were taught to you once you were in a SEAL platoon. There, you learned through a fire hose. There was so much knowledge you needed, so many skills to develop, so many tactics to understand, you felt you would never know it all. But like the rest of the new guys, I listened and I learned. Every single day.

In my first three platoons, I learned a few key concepts that stuck with me for the rest of my career, and they also were the base upon which I built most of the principles I ended up teaching to the rest of the SEAL Teams and, eventually, to companies, businesses, and organizations around the globe. These are examples of the lucky moments I referred to earlier. I was in the right place at the right time, with the right frame of mind to learn what I did. Then I was lucky enough to have other experiences to overlay what I had learned and slowly, subconsciously, begin to formulate a system of leadership that I was then lucky enough to apply on one of the most challenging battlefields in the world—the Battle of Ramadi in the summer of 2006. When I returned from that deployment, I took over the training for the West Coast SEAL Teams, where I formalized, codified, and transcribed what I had learned. But the roots of everything I eventually wrote down originated in a very nontraditional but highly effective learning environment: the SEAL platoon.

PART 1

LEADERSHIP STRATEGIES

FOUNDATIONS

FIRST PLATOON: DETACH

It was in my first platoon that I learned the power of being able to detach myself from the chaos and mayhem going on, take a step back, and see what was actually happening. I was lucky that it happened the way it did.

We were training to assault offshore oil platforms. In the Persian Gulf, oil platforms could be taken over by enemy forces for a variety of reasons, and we would need to be able to take them back. SEALs had participated in operations against Iranian-controlled oil rigs in the region in the 1980s, and the thought was that we might have to do it again. So we trained and prepared to execute that very specific mission.

We would spend time and do training exercises and mock operations on commercial oil platforms in various locations. It was great training, mainly because oil platforms are incredibly complex and dangerous structures. Many parts of an oil platform are highly flammable and under massive pressure, so we had to learn what to be cautious of in the event we ever did a real mission on an oil platform. During a real mission with live ammunition and explosive charges used to open doors, we would obviously need to make sure we understood the danger involved.

But what really makes an oil platform a challenging target is the complexity of the structure itself. It is a maze of stairwells and hallways and rooms and open areas covered with equipment. And, unlike any other target SEALs might encounter, it is a true three-dimensional problem because many of the floors are made of heavy metal grating that you can see through. So it is very difficult to conceal your movement, and the enemy threat is high because the enemy can see you from a great distance away—after all, they can see through the floors too.

As a new guy, I was doing my best, trying to make the right moves at the right time, listening to the tactical calls being made by the leadership, and trying to support those calls. At this point in our predeployment workup cycle, the platoon had already been through a lot together. We had completed a full cycle of land warfare training, done extensive close-quarters combat training, and executed urban training, reconnaissance training, and various air and maritime training. So while I was still a new guy, most of the other new guys and I had certainly begun to understand the tactics we were being taught. As usual for me, my individual skills were nothing special. I was not the best shot, not the fastest at reloading my weapon, and definitely not setting any records on the combat-swimmer training dives we conducted. But I did feel pretty good about the tactics we were shown, how they worked, and how they were applied. I paid close attention to my platoon leadership, watched them make their tactical decisions, and tried to understand why they made the choices they made.

But I was still a new guy. It certainly wasn't my place to make tactical calls or tell people what to do.

Then, during one clearance of the oil rig, something happened that hadn't happened before. As we were moving through the structure, the whole platoon entered an area of the rig and became overwhelmed with what was in front of them. It was a large level of the platform, covered with mechanical gear and equipment, which created numerous hiding areas for enemy personnel and presented a complex tactical problem. The whole platoon stood there, side by side, looking down the sites of our weapons at the potential enemy threats, like an old-fashioned skirmish line.

I stood there like the rest of the platoon, scanning for targets and trying to identify dangerous high-pressure or flammable areas while I waited for a call to be made directing us on our next move.

I waited a little longer, still scanning, thinking someone needed to make a call so we would know what to do next.

I waited even longer. Still nothing. Out of my peripheral vision, I saw the guys to my left and to my right, all doing the same thing I was: holding their weapons in the ready position, scanning for targets, and waiting for the call.

But the call still didn't come. I waited a little longer, until finally,

I had had enough. I elevated my weapon into the "high-port" position, meaning I pointed it in a safe direction toward the sky and away from the threats. Then I took a half step back off the firing line and looked to my left and to my right. It was plain to see: every person in the platoon—including the platoon commander, the platoon chief, the assistant platoon commander, and the leading petty officer—was pointing his weapon toward the threat, scanning for targets. But no one was looking anywhere else. They could only see the field of view down the sights of their weapons; no one had any situational awareness of anything else going on. Yet even as a lowly new guy, I could see the whole situation with complete clarity. When I was on the line looking down my gun, I was only seeing what was directly in my field of fire. Now that I had stepped back and looked around, I could see the entire deck, all its obstacles, and the simplest way to clear it. By stepping back, I had detached myself mentally and physically from the immediate problem, and now it was easy for me to see the solution, clearer than even the more experienced SEALs in my platoon.

I took a breath and paused another second to confirm no one else was going to move, look around, or make a call. No one was moving. The platoon was frozen. I had to do something.

"*Hold left, move right!*" I barked in as authoritative a voice as I could muster. Even as I said it, I half expected someone to look over, see it was me—a new guy trying to make a call—and tell me to shut my mouth.

Instead, each member of the platoon did what we are always

trained to do when we hear a verbal command—they passed the word. *"Hold left, move right!"* *"Hold left, move right!"* the word repeated down the line. As the word was passed, it simultaneously turned into action. The guys on the left side of the deck held their position scanning for targets, covering the threats as the guys on the right began to move to push through and clear the area from the right flank. This was not a complex tactical call; it was a standard cover-and-move procedure that we had practiced and rehearsed countless times. And as soon as the guys heard it, they did it.

As they executed the movement, I realized something very powerful. I realized that by high porting my weapon, stepping back off the firing line, and looking around—by detaching physically, even if only by a few inches, and, more important, detaching mentally from the problem at hand—I was able to see infinitely more than anyone else in my platoon. And since I was able to see everything, I was able to make a good decision, which allowed me, a new guy and the most junior guy in the platoon, to lead. The cellar deck was soon cleared, and we continued moving through the rig, clearing the remaining levels. No one complained or objected to my decision, and once we'd completed the run, one of the more senior guys actually told me I had made a good call.

My platoon's reaction reinforced this idea of detaching, and I began to do it as often as I could. It wasn't easy. Sometimes, I would still get caught up focusing on the things immediately in front of me. But at a minimum, I became aware of it. Then I made it my goal to never be completely caught up in the minuscule tactical aspects of a problem; my goal was to get to a higher mental and physical altitude to see more. Just as it had worked on the oil rig, detachment worked in land warfare, in close-quarters combat, and in the urban training areas. It worked in every simulated combat environment we were put in. The more often I detached, the easier it became to see and understand the tactical picture, and the better I got at it.

As I got older, increased in rank, and was put into actual designated leadership positions, detaching became one of the foundations of my leadership style. Eventually, I realized that detaching not only worked in tactical scenarios, but in life. When having a conversation with someone, I realized that if I detached, I could better read their emotions and their reactions. I also realized that if I was able to detach, I could better assess and manage *my own* emotions and reactions. When I became an assistant platoon commander, platoon commander, and task unit commander, I learned to detach myself from the mission-planning process so I would not be caught up in the details and so I would be able to see the bigger picture and come across as the tactical genius that had all the answers.

Detachment is one of the most powerful tools a leader can have. The question is, pragmatically, how do you do it?

Step one is to be aware. Pay attention to yourself and what is happening around you. Make it a goal to avoid being fully absorbed in the minute details of any situation. Don't let it happen. If you are staying aware, checking yourself, you will be likelier to avoid getting tunnel vision.

Listen to indicators like your breath, your voice. Are you breathing hard? Are you raising your voice? Be aware of your body. Are you clenching your teeth? Squeezing your fists?

All these reactions are signs of getting emotional about the situation. When that happens, or when a situation is becoming chaotic, step back. Physically take a step back. Lift your chin up, which elevates your vision and compels you to look around. Once you are physically detached from the situation, this cues you to do the same thing mentally. Take a deep breath and exhale. Look methodically from the left to the right and back again. This is another cue from your body to your mind to relax, look around, absorb what you are seeing, let go of your emotions, and make a dispassionate and accurate assessment of the situation so you can make a good decision.

When you begin to follow these steps and detach, you will see it is one of the most powerful tools a leader can have.

Of course, there is a dichotomy to detachment that must be balanced. You can take it too far; you can become so detached that you lose the connection to what is happening. This is unusual, but if it does happen—if you begin to lose touch with your scenario—don't fret. Just take a step back in, get a little closer to the problem, and engage.

SECOND PLATOON: ARROGANCE AND HUMILITY

Once you finish your first deployment as a new guy, you aren't a new guy anymore. As you are assigned to your second platoon, you graduate from "new guy" to a "one-cruise wonder," which means you might not be a new guy anymore, but you still don't know everything—although you think you might.

There was a solid contingent of one-cruise wonders in my second platoon at SEAL Team One. The team had kept a bunch of us together from our previous platoon and then added some of the other one-cruise wonders from some of the other platoons. Our platoon chief was actually a senior chief, who was very smart and experienced, as was our leading petty officer (LPO). We also happened to have an incredibly talented leader as our assistant platoon commander, the Navy Midshipmen record-setting quarterback Alton Lee Grizzard. Not only was he overflowing with natural leadership capability, he had deployed already and taken part in real-world operations in Somalia.

So the platoon leadership was very strong. All except for the actual platoon commander himself. He had done a lateral transfer from another occupational specialty in the navy to become a SEAL. This meant that even though he was a senior lieutenant, he was very inexperienced in the SEAL Teams. He had not done a SEAL Team workup or a deployment yet. He did not have the experience a platoon commander would normally have. And yet he was in charge of the platoon.

That alone is not a big deal; the military is set up to work that way. An inexperienced officer is surrounded by solid senior enlisted personnel who give the officer tactical guidance and keep things running smoothly. At least that is the way it is supposed to work. But in this platoon, it wasn't working that way at all.

In this particular case, the platoon commander did not want to listen to advice from his senior enlisted leadership or from any of us. Even though he was the least experienced individual in the platoon besides the new guys, he wanted to make all the decisions. All the plans were *his* plans. All the decisions were *his* decisions. He didn't want to listen to anyone.

Needless to say, this did not go over very well. Not only did it rub the senior enlisted leadership the wrong way, when the rest of us troops saw that he did not take input from the senior enlisted leadership, it made us nervous. If he wasn't listening to the advice being offered from the most experienced guys in the platoon, we worried his plans might be suspect. We were right. The plans the platoon commander created and imposed on us were not good, and it showed. We had some issues out in the field. We didn't accomplish our training missions at the level we should have.

But our subpar performance didn't change the attitude of the platoon commander. When we failed a training mission, he blamed others. He would never recognize or admit that perhaps his plan wasn't the best or maybe the decisions he'd made in the field weren't good calls.

Looking back, it is obvious that what this officer lacked in experience, he made up for with a massive ego. I didn't fully understand this at the time; I just didn't have the experience to recognize what was going on. But it is clear now that he lacked any level of humility whatsoever.

I have to give credit to my senior chief and leading petty officer. We young enlisted guys watched as our senior enlisted leaders did their best to counsel, cajole, influence, and mentor. They spent extra time explaining how things worked. They tried to get him to put his ego in check and let some of them make some of the tactical decisions.

Unfortunately, they failed to change him. Months went by, and there was no improvement in the platoon commander's behavior. Finally, one late night before an arduous training mission out in the desert, our LPO, the second most senior enlisted man in the platoon, had had enough. He disagreed with the platoon commander's plan, and he let him know it. The disagreement escalated into an argument, then into a full-on yelling match, and finally, the platoon commander snapped and took a swing at the LPO. We all jumped in and separated the two, but it was a bad scene.

It should be known that there are certainly a fair share of friendly scraps in a healthy SEAL platoon. Verbal jousting often leads to a round of good-natured fisticuffs or a perhaps a lighthearted grappling match. But this fight was different. There was no playing around in this situation. And even worse, it was an officer taking a swing at an enlisted man.

Over the next few days, a dark mood fell over the platoon. We realized we had a real problem. Our officer was arrogant and not listening to anyone. That was bad enough. But now he had tried to hit our LPO. This was unacceptable. We wouldn't stand for it. The grumblings about the situation turned into a roar, and our disorganized complaints became organized. We needed to make a stand.

We had some closed-door meetings among the enlisted men. We consulted our senior chief and LPO, and eventually we decided we would go to see our commanding officer and tell him we didn't want to work for our platoon commander. We wanted him gone. This was a mutiny.

Now, I don't want to make this sound more dramatic than it was, but according to the Uniform Code of Military Justice, which is the legal code by which military members must abide: "A person who is found guilty of attempted mutiny, mutiny, sedition, or failure to report a mutiny or sedition shall be punished by death." And this is what we were doing—revolting against our leader. Of course, this was peacetime, and there was zero chance of the situation escalating into a criminal mutiny where we would be taken to court-martial, but it was a serious situation to have enlisted troops asking to have their platoon commander fired.

A couple of days later, we got back to the team from the desert training area. Our senior chief talked to the master chief of the command, the senior enlisted man at SEAL Team One, and explained the situation. He got us a meeting with the commanding officer of SEAL Team One.

Our commanding officer was a highly respected leader. He was down-to-earth and charismatic, with a great reputation as a tactical operator—a rare reputation for a senior officer to have.

When scheduled, the enlisted men of our platoon reported to the commanding officer's office. He called us in and asked us individually to explain the situation. Once by one, we told him our versions of what we had seen the night the platoon commander tried to hit our LPO, and we detailed the general atmosphere of the platoon. I told him, "The platoon commander doesn't really listen to anyone else. It's his way or the highway."

The commanding officer listened intently. I thought he was on board with what we were saying, but after the last man had spoken, he looked up and down the line and said, "Listen up, boys. I get that the situation might not be ideal. It sounds like there are some personality conflicts. But this also sounds like a mutiny. *And we don't allow mutinies in the navy.* So stop it. Go back to your platoon. Get to work. And figure this out. Understand?"

"Yes, sir," we all replied.

It made sense. We had spoken our minds, and we were told to get back in line. We did. Because we had such respect for the commanding officer, we didn't question what he said. He told us to get back in line, and we did. We went down to our platoon space and got back to work.

The commanding officer had squashed our rebellion. He was right; mutinies are not allowed in the navy, and he wasn't going to have one at his SEAL Team.

But it turns out, he also wasn't going to have a bad platoon commander. Over the next couple of days, the commanding officer consulted with the command master chief, talked more with our platoon senior chief, did a thorough assessment of the platoon commander's leadership shortfalls, and, based on that assessment, called our platoon commander into the commanding officer's office and relieved him of his duties as platoon commander. It wasn't a mutiny from the troops; it was a decision by the commanding officer. The platoon commander was removed from his position and removed from SEAL Team One.

This alone might have been a good leadership lesson for me as a young SEAL: arrogance and throwing rank around does not work. But I'm not sure if I would have really understood that lesson had it not been for what happened next.

With the old platoon commander fired, we got a new platoon commander, and he was the complete opposite of his predecessor. Everyone in the SEAL Teams had heard of our new platoon commander. He went by his initials, but from the phonetic alphabet: Delta Charlie.

Delta Charlie had an incredible reputation as an officer and as an enlisted man. He had started his career as an enlisted man and risen through the ranks all the way to senior chief, the second from the top enlisted rank in the navy, just beneath master chief. He had then earned his commission and become an officer. In his career, he had been assigned to every job a SEAL could have. He had initially been at the old Underwater Demolition Team before they were decommissioned and turned into SEAL Teams. He had been a plank owner at Richard Marcinko's SEAL Team. He was stationed at a regular SEAL Team, the Special Boat Team, served as an instructor at BUD/S, and even the SEAL Delivery Vehicle Team, home of Naval Special Warfare Command's mini-submarines.

On top of all that, he had combat experience. He had participated in the invasion of Grenada as a member of the element tasked with taking control of the country's main radio tower. We didn't know much about that operation, but we knew one thing: it was real, and none of us had done anything real.

As I heard about Delta Charlie taking over, I was excited but also intimidated. After all, as a one-cruise wonder, I thought I had some knowledge, but I didn't think that knowledge would stack up against that possessed by someone like Delta Charlie, who had infinitely more experience than I or anyone else in the platoon had. I also imagined that Delta Charlie was assigned this platoon to straighten us out, to ensure this young group of mutineers was put in its place. I figured we were in for some stern leadership and strict control after our rebellion. I braced for impact.

Then I met Delta Charlie for the first time. He was not what I'd expected at all. He was smaller than I'd imagined, standing about five foot seven or so, and had a fairly lean build, probably weighing in at around 165 pounds, give or take.

He also had a relaxed way about him. He seemed very calm, usually carrying a half smile on his face. When he spoke to us for the first time, he said, "I'm looking forward to working *with* all of you."

That was the first indicator of what kind of a leader Delta Charlie was going to be. It was subtle, but I noticed it. He didn't say, "I'm looking forward to leading you," or "I'm glad to be taking over this platoon," or "I run a tight ship," or even "I'm honored to be taking over as your commander." Instead, he said he was looking forward to working *with* us all—his use of the word *with* standing in stark contrast to what we had been hearing from the old platoon commander, who always separated himself from us in his speech. But Delta Charlie was different; he indicated not that he was above us or separate from us but that he was one of us.

But the contrast between Delta Charlie and his predecessor went way beyond that. These two men were diametrically opposed in every possible way, and this was lucky for me, because the contrast between these two leaders was so stark, it left an impression on me and impacted my actions as a leader for the rest of my life.

One of the biggest differences between Delta Charlie and his predecessor was that Delta Charlie had a massive amount of experience, while the former platoon commander had next to none, like the rest of the new guys. Delta Charlie had done everything; the former platoon commander had done nothing. Since Delta Charlie had so much experience, I expected him to tell us exactly how to do everything. After all, that is what the old platoon commander had done, despite his lack of experience and knowledge. The former platoon commander had always come up with his own plan, told us how he wanted us to execute it, and expected us to execute it based on those specific orders.

So I found it quite shocking, as did the rest of the enlisted men in the platoon, that Delta Charlie didn't order us around at all. He didn't come up with his own plans for everything. He didn't tell us how he wanted us to do things. He executed classic Decentralized

Command: he told us what needed to get done and then told us to go figure out how we wanted to do it. And when I say *us*, I am not only talking about the senior enlisted personnel; I am talking about us junior enlisted personnel as well. He would tell me or a few of the other junior guys, "Hey, here is the mission for tonight. Figure out how you think we should do it and let me know."

We were nervous, but thrilled. We wanted to do a good job, and we put our utmost effort into coming up with a tactically sound plan. Once we had one, we would present it to Delta Charlie. Inevitably, he would find some mistakes in it, which he would point out to us. I was always impressed that we could spend four or five hours poring over the presumptive operation, staring at the map, discussing and poking holes in our ideas, and when we would finally present the plan to Delta Charlie, he would quickly assess it and point out a few problems. It was amazing. He seemed like a tactical genius. But what I realized later was that he was detached from the planning process, so he could see it from altitude and easily see where the holes were.

This is the exact opposite thing from what would happen when our former platoon commander would come up with a plan on his own and then force it down upon us. When that happened, we were the ones seeing the holes in his plan, and we couldn't fathom how he could come up with such a horrible one.

On top of that, when Delta Charlie would allow us to come up with the plan, we would have complete ownership of it. Of course we did; it was *our plan*. He didn't need to convince us to buy into it; we had already bought in. And when we would go into the field to execute the plan, since it was *our* plan, we were completely committed to making it a success. When we would hit an obstacle, we would find a way around it, over it, or through it. We would stop at nothing to execute the plan and accomplish the mission.

That attitude was totally contrary to how we felt about the former platoon commander's plans. They were *his* plans, not ours, so we didn't have ownership of them, and it was a struggle for him to get us to buy into them. After all, we are humans with our own ideas, and because of our egos, we often think our ideas are the best. When he imposed a plan on us, we would automatically think of how much better our own plan would be, and we kept that in the backs of our heads, especially when we went into the field. When we hit an obstacle, instead of trying to figure out a way to overcome it, we simply thought, *The platoon commander didn't think of this, did he? His plan is awful! My plan would have been much better.* Without everyone buying into the plan, taking ownership, and making every possible effort to ensure it was carried out and the mission accomplished, there was a good chance it would fail.

There was another thing Delta Charlie did that made an impression on me: he took out the trash. This is no big deal, and I likely wouldn't have thought too much about it, except for the fact that I never saw the former platoon commander do it. You see, the platoon office—or, as it is called in the SEAL Teams, the *platoon hut*—needs to be cleaned every day. This assignment usually goes to the new guys. At the end of every day, the new guys sweep up, dust off, and take out the trash. Cleaning is a menial but necessary task, and it keeps the new guys humble. As a one-cruise wonder, I felt like I was way above cleaning up; I didn't need to do that anymore. And the higher up you went in the chain of command, it seemed to me the more distance there was from the menial task of cleaning up.

Unless you were Delta Charlie. At the end of each day, he would take out the trash. Maybe run a broom through the space. It was no big deal; it took him less than two minutes to push the broom, then consolidate the trash from the two or three garbage cans in the platoon space, take them outside, and throw them in the dumpster. But those two minutes left a mark on me. This was a tangible and physical action that represented pure humility. Delta Charlie was the *most senior man* in the platoon; he also had *the most experience.* But there he was, taking out the garbage. And yet I was too good to do it?

We only had to see that a couple of times before the other lower enlisted guys and I started preemptively taking out the trash and cleaning the space so Delta Charlie didn't have to. We did it out of respect—respect that Delta Charlie didn't demand, but earned.

The former platoon commander, on the other hand, had eschewed any kind of menial labor. It was below him. He was the almighty platoon commander, the officer in charge; he wasn't going to *take out garbage.* And when he acted that way, *well, we weren't going to take out his garbage either.* None of the lower enlisted guys did anything to help him out. He was on his own.

And while Delta Charlie was a phenomenal tactician, an incredible planner, and a gifted operator, it was his humility more than anything else that drove the platoon to want to do a good job for him. We didn't want to let him down. We didn't want to disappoint him in any way. And we certainly didn't want to make him look anything less than perfect to our commanding officer. So we worked as hard as we could in everything we did. Everything. And this dedication showed in the way the platoon performed; it was the best platoon I was ever a part of.

That platoon changed the course of my life, and Delta Charlie had an immense impact on me, because when you are a young SEAL in a SEAL platoon, that SEAL platoon is your whole world. In that platoon, under the original platoon commander, our world was miserable. But when Delta Charlie came in and took over, almost instantly our whole world was good. That was one of the strongest displays of the impact of leadership I had ever seen. I thought at the time, *Delta Charlie just made the world good for this whole platoon. One day, if I can, I am going to try to make the world good for sixteen SEALs in a platoon.* And it was that thought right there that started me on the path to becoming an officer.

The core of what Delta Charlie taught me was the importance of humility. He had all that experience and all that knowledge and the rank and the position; he had every reason to elevate himself above us, every reason to look down on us, every reason to act as if he were better than everyone else, but he never looked down on us at all. The fact that he didn't is what made us respect him and want, *truly want,* to follow him. I still try to follow his example to this day.

THIRD PLATOON:
OVERSTEPPING MY BOUNDS

In my third platoon, our core group of guys stuck together once again. We knew one another well, trusted one another, and we operated together like a close-knit team. As happened with every platoon at that time, once we got back from deployment with Delta Charlie as our platoon commander, we got a new platoon commander. He was a solid guy with a good reputation, and we liked him a lot. Of course, he had big shoes to fill, and he knew that, but it didn't bother him. He didn't make any attempts to be Delta Charlie; instead, he just forged his own path and led with his strengths, which worked out fine. Even though he didn't have the experience Delta Charlie did, by that point, we lower enlisted guys had learned so much from Delta Charlie that we could make a lot of things happen on our own. The new platoon commander knew that and was good with it.

We had a good workup, which is what we called our predeployment training cycle, and then we were sent on deployment overseas on board a U.S. Navy ship. There was no war going on, so we worked in other countries, either training the host nation military or finding training to do on our own.

At one point, we left the ship and went into the desert in a country in the Persian Gulf region to conduct unilateral training, meaning it was just us—no foreign counterparts or other American forces. We set up some land warfare training in the middle of the desert to run some refresher exercises for our immediate action drills—or

IADs—for land warfare. IADs are the preplanned movements a SEAL platoon will execute when contacted by the enemy, almost like preplanned plays run by a football team. There are multiple predesignated calls that are used to give instructions to the members of the platoon for what maneuver is to be executed: flanking the enemy, breaking contact, getting on line, or moving forward, backward, left, or right. These calls are usually made by the platoon commander or the platoon chief, depending on where the enemy is located.

In this particular drill, we were patrolling when we were "attacked" by the enemy. All that actually meant was that we spotted some man-shaped silhouette targets that had been set up, and we started shooting at them. As the radioman, I was toward the front of the platoon, just behind the platoon commander, who follows behind the point man.

When the shooting started, we all dropped into our fields of fire, just as we had trained countless times before. I quickly scanned my field of fire, then mentally detached and started to swivel my head and look around to assess the situation. We were slightly behind a small sand berm, which provided most of us with good, solid cover. I was out of danger, so I elevated my head a bit to take a better look. I saw that the berm actually provided a good escape route, and we could simply peel behind it one man at a time.

I waited for the platoon commander to make the call, but he didn't. I waited a little bit longer. Still no call. Because I was detached and out of "danger" behind the berm, I knew exactly what had to happen. The call needed to come out, but it still didn't. Another second or two went by, and I finally shouted, *"Peel right!"* As we are trained, everyone passed the word, and we commenced the peel right maneuver.

It went smoothly; it was one of the most basic calls and simplest maneuvers we trained to do. A few minutes later, after we had put a couple of hundred meters between us and the "enemy contact," we formed a hasty perimeter, set 360-degree security, redistributed ammunition, confirmed our head count, and then called cease-fire and ENDEX, which meant *end of the exercise.*

We did a quick debrief. The platoon commander seemed frustrated.

"What were you doing making that call?" he asked.

"No call was being made, so I just made it. 'In the absence of orders, lead!'" I said, quoting an old military leadership maxim.

"There was no absence of orders. I was assessing. I wanted to assault through the enemy. You spoke too soon," he told me. He didn't make that big of a deal out of it, but I could certainly sense he wasn't happy with what I had done.

It would have been easy for me to get defensive and attack the platoon commander. "You weren't making a call, and someone had to!" I could have told him. But that was wrong. Instead, I realized I had made a mistake. It wasn't a grievous error, but I had overstepped my bounds, and doing that had a negative effect on the situation because we hadn't executed what the platoon commander had intended. But it had a positive effect on me because it taught me a lesson. From that moment on, I realized I didn't always need to lead. I didn't need to be at the center of decision-making. I realized it was my job to support the team and the mission, which meant supporting the boss.

I learned this lesson relatively painlessly, but as I continued in the SEAL Teams, I saw the same type of mistake manifest itself in awful ways as egos clashed over who was in charge, who made calls, who led, and who followed. I saw people throughout my career—and still see it today in the business world—jockeying for position and maneuvering against one another rather than maneuvering against the enemy.

I learned that day that even though I had to be ready to lead, I also had to know when to follow—and that to be a good leader, I had to be a good follower. I learned to subordinate my ego to the mission and to my boss. Does that mean I am weak? No, it means I put the team and the mission above myself so that we can win. And that simple lesson played out thousands of times throughout my career.

LAWS OF COMBAT AND PRINCIPLES OF LEADERSHIP

I learned countless other lessons along the way over the following years and deployments. The lessons were tested during my last deployment, where I led SEAL Team Three, Task Unit Bruiser, in the Battle of Ramadi. That deployment is where most of the combat examples Leif Babin and I wrote about in *Extreme Ownership* and

The Dichotomy of Leadership come from. But the principles were not fully crystallized until I took over the tactical training for the West Coast SEAL Teams. That training is not individual training, where lone SEALs learn individual skills like sniping or combat trauma care, but collective training, where SEALs work together as platoons and task units to hash out their standard operating procedures and learn to integrate together to accomplish their missions. This is the training where SEALs learn to shoot, move, and communicate; where they learn to close with and destroy the enemy; and where they learn combat leadership.

The training I ran covers all tactical environments. There is work in rural terrain, such as deserts, forests, or mountains. There is work in urban environments like cities and villages, and close quarters inside buildings of all shapes and sizes. During this training, SEALs learn to transit great distances over the ocean in small boats, or under the ocean on rebreathing scuba gear. They jump out of airplanes, rappel from helicopters, and learn and rehearse the tactics of fighting with and from vehicles in formation. They do all these things together as a team.

The end of each block of training consists of what we call an *FTX phase. FTX* stands for *field training exercise,* and it consists of full-mission profiles, where the SEAL task units conduct the entire progression of mock operations—from planning to rehearsals, insertion, infiltration, and actions at the objective on the target itself, followed by exfiltration and extraction back to base. Once back at base, they will go through the drills of analyzing the intelligence they gathered and using that intelligence to plan and prepare for follow-on training operations.

The FTX phase usually consists of about five to seven days of continuous operations. Sleep is limited, and stress is high. The planning cycle is short and demands good foresight and organization. Once the platoons are in the field, stress is maximized.

The training cadre goes to great lengths to simulate combat. Platoons are loaded out with Simunition paintball rounds, or a multimillion-dollar laser tag system that mounts on the SEALs' real weapons. The laser tag system also requires the SEALs to wear sensors that detect when they are being shot; when "hit," the sensor vest also has small speakers that announce what type of wound the SEAL has suffered or if the SEAL has been killed. The speakers also provide sound effects of bullets snapping overhead or whizzing close by or explosions going off in the area.

The paintball and laser systems allow SEALs to actively fight against other SEALs who role-play as the bad guys—or as we call them, *OPFOR*—which is short for *opposing force*. The OPFOR are experienced SEAL-training cadre who know the SEAL tactics. Without questions, they are the toughest enemy the SEAL platoons and task units will ever face.

In addition to the OPFOR, who dress up in enemy garb, there are other things the training cadre does to make the training realistic. They use professional set designers to make the training areas look like Iraq, Afghanistan, or any other locale the SEALs might be fighting in. The buildings are given façades and other treatment to make them resemble the architecture and construction materials seen overseas. There are street signs and graffiti written in foreign languages. Even entire markets are assembled, complete with local goods ready to be bought or traded.

Also inserted into those scenes are other role-players besides the OPFOR, who do not play hostile insurgents or terrorists but innocent civilians. For those characters, the training cadre hires ethnic actors and actresses who not only look and dress the part but also speak the language, creating another obstacle for the SEALs going through the training.

The final component in creating stress is the use of special effects and pyrotechnics. Explosions, smoke, fire, rockets, grenades, and simulated improvised explosive devices are utilized to cause stress and add to the realism of the scenario.

With all these elements combined, the training is extremely realistic. Looking through night vision goggles and seeing the detail on the buildings, the people moving around, and the explosions going off, it isn't hard to slip into the mind-set that you aren't training at all—you are at war.

This was the training I took charge of when I came back from the Battle of Ramadi. Within a few days of taking over the training, fresh off the battlefield myself, I went out to the desert to observe a SEAL task unit going through its land warfare FTX phase.

It was an absolute disaster. A complete and utter failure.

I was apprehensive as I watched the members plan. The situation was extremely complex; they had been tasked with hitting a target in the desert that consisted of one large building in a small valley surrounded by six smaller buildings. They had broken their force into six different elements, each of which was approaching the target from a different direction. While it seemed like the best way to isolate the target and mitigate the opportunities for someone to escape from it, it was also very complicated. It minimized the ability of the teams to support or even communicate with one another. When teams are split apart, confusion can easily ensue. When teams are split into six different elements, that confusion is multiplied. *Keep things simple* is an ancient military maxim that holds true for any type of planning. This task unit was failing to keep things simple.

Once out on target, things got even worse. The assault commenced, and almost immediately, some of the elements were pinned down by enemy fire. But because of their distance from the other SEAL elements, they could not be supported. None of the other elements could provide cover fire, which meant the elements that were pinned down could not move. When they did try to move without any cover fire, they suffered more casualties. This was a lesson I had learned from the Vietnam SEALs who put me through training, a lesson that was reinforced in everything we did in the SEAL Teams: Cover and Move. If you are going to move, you must have someone covering for you, protecting you. This can mean someone actually actively shooting to keep the enemy's heads down, or someone in a good position, actively scanning for enemy personnel to appear as you move. This is the fundamental tactic of everything we do as SEALs.

If we are in a shooting pair—just two men—and we have to secure a prisoner, one SEAL keeps his weapon trained on the enemy while the other SEAL maneuvers to take physical control of the prisoner. If the prisoner makes a move, the SEAL on his gun can eliminate the threat.

If a platoon is doing a "danger crossing"—that is, crossing a road or a river, we always bring up additional security to hold down the road and make sure no enemy approaches—and if enemy does approach, the additional security are ready to engage and cover the movement of the platoon across the open area.

As we move down a hallway, there are always one or two SEALs with their weapons trained down the length of it, covering the movement of the rest of the platoon.

If we are operating in fire teams in a rural environment, while one team is moving, the other fire team is putting down suppressive fire or at least scanning the terrain for the enemy. The same thing happens during a target assault; one team sets up a base position and puts down heavy suppressive fire while the other team moves through the target, and as they move through, the base element shifts fire, staying ahead of the maneuver element.

Cover and Move is even utilized at a larger scale; as a platoon or task unit moves to a target area, there is often an aircraft overhead, covering by watching with powerful optical sensors, scanning the area, and ready to provide fire support if necessary.

But on this particular FTX, the various elements were not able to cover for one another at all.

On top of that, one of the larger elements got bogged down in confronting multiple problems in the large main building of the target. They were being shot at with paintballs from multiple directions, and some of the men had already been wounded. There were multiple innocent civilians scared and screaming for help, and the leader did not know where all his men were, so he didn't want to exit the building for fear of leaving someone behind.

I stood watching the leader. He was trying to get his wounded men tended to. He was trying to get a good head count. He was trying to get control of the civilians. Lastly, he was trying to figure out where his element was getting shot at from. What he didn't seem to realize was that if he didn't stop the enemy from shooting at him—if he didn't win that firefight or at least suppress the enemy fire—none of his other problems were going to matter because they would all be dead. He kept trying to do too many things simultaneously, and by trying to do everything, he was accomplishing nothing. He needed to figure out his biggest priority problem and execute a plan to fix that problem before moving on to the next one. He needed to Prioritize and Execute.

As he tried to lead his troops to do what he wanted, he was giving out long, intricate, and complicated instructions. With those complex instructions added to the existing chaos and confusion, no one really understood what he wanted them to do. His language was too convoluted. Without understanding what he wanted them to do, there was no possible way the troops could execute. Again, he needed to *Keep things simple*—in this case, his language.

Those complex orders also revealed the final problem I noticed: everyone on the team was waiting to be told what to do. The platoon commanders were waiting for direction from the task unit commander. The squad leaders were waiting for a call from the platoon commanders, the fire team leaders were waiting for orders from the squad leaders, and the individual SEALs—the machine gunners and assaulters, the corpsman and the radioman, everyone—they were all waiting to be told what to do. All direction was stemming only from the most senior leader; all command was centralized. As they waited for orders, they froze and did nothing.

But what they all needed to do was take initiative; they needed to make things happen. They needed to understand the broad direction from the boss, and then they needed to act. What they needed was Decentralized Command.

Soon it was clear the task unit was completely combat ineffective, so I told the OPFOR to back off and not commence any further attacks. The task unit was broken, and its members wallowed in their misery as they slowly pulled together enough of a plan to carry their dead and wounded off the battlefield to the extraction point. It was a brutal struggle to accomplish this, as more than half the task unit were "casualties." Carrying two- to three-hundred-pound bodies over steep and rough terrain for four or five hours gave the members plenty of time to think about what they had done wrong.

It gave me plenty of time to think as well.

The thing that stood out to me more than anything else was that the whole reason this task unit had failed so miserably was because of one thing and one thing only: leadership.

Then I realized that of everything I was responsible for teaching these SEALs, far and away, the most important thing I needed to teach them was how to lead. I needed to take the lessons I had learned in my career, lessons that could be traced back to our Vietnam SEAL forefathers who had brought back lessons from their time in combat. Lessons that I had deployed with to Iraq and had been crystallized by the crucible of sustained combat. I needed to take those lessons and distill them down into something these young SEAL leaders could easily understand and implement in their platoons and task units.

When I got back to the barracks that night, I sat down at a table in the chow hall and wrote down what I believed to be the most important and fundamental principles of combat leadership, what I would eventually call the Laws of Combat:

- *Cover and Move*
- *Simple*
- *Prioritize and Execute*
- *Decentralized Command*

Cover and Move came first because it is the root of all other tactics and because it is teamwork. A unit in the field by itself is a fraction of what it is when it has another unit supporting it. Two teams working together, covering and moving for each other, don't just double their effectiveness; they multiply their impact and capability exponentially. Without coordination and cooperation between individuals, between elements within a team, and between teams, all is lost.

One the severest warnings I used to give SEAL fire teams, squads, platoons, and task units was to maintain a *supporting distance* between elements—a doctrinal term that for small units means the distance between two units that can be covered effectively by their fires. I would add to this that the distance must be able to be covered by primary or at least secondary communications. That way, each element can get help if they need it. As soon as an element is out of supporting distance, they are all but doomed. So Cover and Move—teamwork—is the highest priority in the Laws of Combat.

Next is Simple. Once we have established the ability to Cover and Move—we have a team that can work together—then we need a simple and distinct goal. Everyone on the team must understand that goal. It must be clear. In addition to the goal being simple and clear, plans and directives must be communicated up and down the chain of command in a simple, clear, concise manner that can be comprehended by everyone. Simplicity is key, because if the team members cannot understand the goal or the plan to accomplish that goal, there is no possible way they can execute. So keep it Simple.

The next law is Prioritize and Execute. There will be multiple tasks that need to be accomplished or numerous problems that must be solved. If the leader or the team members try to accomplish too many things at once, they will likely accomplish nothing. The most impactful task or the biggest problem must be addressed first, then the next, then the next, and so on until everything is handled.

The final law is Decentralized Command. For a team to utilize Decentralized Command, it must implement the other laws. Then Decentralized Command comes to life; everyone on the team must step up and lead.

A task unit has eight four- or five-man fire teams in it. Each of those fire teams has a leader. I used to ask the task unit commanders, "What if each of those fire team leaders clearly knew what your intent was and what you wanted the task unit to accomplish, and they took initiative to make that intent come to fruition?" It was a rhetorical question, because they knew the answer. If the fire team leaders were moving their teams toward the commander's broad goal on their own initiative, things would be fairly easy for the task unit commander.

But that all hinged on the task unit commander simply and clearly conveying his intent. Only if the fire team leaders understood that intent could they execute anything. And their execution also depended on their confidence to make decisions and the level of empowerment they felt. Only if the fire team leaders felt they were empowered to make things happen would they step up and lead. That empowerment had to be ingrained in the minds of the subordinate leaders; it had to be imbedded in the culture of the team.

Those four concepts, Cover and Move, Simple, Prioritize and Execute, and Decentralized Command, are the four Laws of Combat, and they work. I saw it over and over again. As the SEAL platoons and task units improved their ability to implement these laws through the various blocks of training, their ability to accomplish tasks and overcome problems improved, and eventually the units that got really good could defeat the OPFOR regardless of what the OPFOR did.

Conversely, when a task unit failed to learn to utilize these laws, it failed its missions. And its failures always tied directly back into the failure of the unit to follow or effectively implement one or more of the laws. The laws were solid, but they were not easy to master. Mastery took training and required failures. But once the laws took root, they worked.

There were two more components of leadership that I solidified during my time as the commander of the training detachment: Extreme Ownership and the Dichotomy of Leadership.

Extreme Ownership is a mind-set of not making excuses and not blaming anyone or anything else when problems occur. Instead of casting blame or making excuses, good leaders and good teams take Extreme Ownership of the problems, find solutions, and implement those solutions. Failure to take ownership results in problems never being solved and teams never improving.

The Dichotomy of Leadership describes opposing forces that are pulling leaders in contradictory directions at the same time. Any trait, technique, or attitude can easily go too far in one direction or the other. To lead properly, a leader must be balanced. For example, leaders must talk, but if they talk too much, they overwhelm their subordinates with information. On the other hand, if they talk too little, the troops aren't properly informed. So the leader has to balance between talking too much and talking too little. A leader must be aggressive, but if they are too aggressive, they might expose themselves to unnecessary risk. Contrarily, if they are not aggressive enough, they will never make progress. So once again, a leader has to be balanced. This list of dichotomies goes on indefinitely, and the answer is always that a leader must maintain balance.

As I watched platoons go through training, I saw over and over again the importance of both Extreme Ownership and the Dichotomy of Leadership. These principles were the cement that held the Laws of Combat together as platoons dealt with arduous training and combat scenarios.

But the laws and the principles didn't only apply to tactical leadership on the battlefield. The more deeply I understood the Laws of Combat, the more I saw them in everything I did. I saw them on the jiu-jitsu mats. I saw them in my family life. And I saw that the Laws of Combat also applied to all leadership—maneuvering through intricate relationships, building coalitions, and getting people to buy into plans and ideas. Dealing with egos and personalities. Understanding and influencing people and teams. The same laws applied.

And just as the laws were difficult to master from a tactical perspective on the battlefield, they are equally difficult to master in noncombat leadership situations. But the more a leader sees the Laws of Combat, the more angles from which a leader can look at them, the better the leader will comprehend and be able to implement the laws and the principles of Extreme Ownership and the Dichotomy of Leadership.

THE POWER OF RELATIONSHIPS

There is another key element to leading any exceptional team: relationships. Leadership requires relationships; good relationships with people above you, below you, and beside you in the chain of command are critical for a strong team. The better the relationships, the more open and effective communication there is. The more communication there is, the stronger the team will be.

For example, there are times when a boss is driving forward on a less-than-ideal path and needs to be redirected. If you have a good relationship with the boss, you can explain, tactfully, what you see to be errors in their thoughts and ideas. As always, the approach you use to discuss this is important. Put the onus on yourself as to why the idea doesn't make sense. For example: "You know, boss, I really want to support the plan to the best of my ability, but I'm having a hard time understanding how to execute this part of it. Can you explain why you want it done that way so I can do it right?" Now the conversation is open, and you can begin to figure out why the boss's idea is what it is and what you can do to influence that idea.

But before even getting to that point, ask yourself some simple questions. First, how much will be gained by approaching the boss and trying to convince them to change their plan? If the difference is minimal, it is probably not worth investing any time or effort into it. Next, ask yourself how much of your concern is just *your* ego; there is a chance that you see *your* way of doing something as "smarter" or "more efficient" than what the boss has offered. If that is the case, and you don't truly think there is much to be gained by using your method, let it go. Don't create drama over your ego. Lastly, ask yourself if you will be moving your relationship with your boss forward or backward by raising this issue. This is important because you should be constantly trying to build that relationship. You are not building the relationship so you can garner favor from the boss; no, you are trying to build a relationship so the boss trusts you and will listen to you so you and the team can more effectively accomplish the mission. For these reasons, choose your battles carefully.

It is obvious that building a trustworthy relationship with your superiors is important. But how do you do that? One of the simplest ways is obvious, but it often gets overlooked—that is performance. Your boss expects you to complete certain tasks. So *complete them.* Do them on time, on budget, and with as little drama as possible. Get the mission done. This includes doing things you might not be in 100 percent agreement with. I did this throughout my career, and it always served me well. Boss wants me to fill out some extra paperwork? I'll do it. Boss needs me to cover a shift for someone else on the team? I've got it. Boss needs someone to clean up an administrative mess that got spilled? I'm on it. Boss has a nasty, low-reward mission that needs executing? I'm all over it.

With each of those problems, I am the solution. With each problem I solve, the level of trust the boss has in me goes up. And I will continue on that path. I won't complain or try to shift bad jobs onto someone else or even look for some kind of praise. I will simply put my head down and do the work. Over time, my boss will know that I am the person who can make things happen. And more important, I gain clout with the boss. This is the opposite of the subordinate who complains and objects or always thinks he has a better way to do things; he loses influence with the boss every time he opens his mouth. Any objection from that subordinate is seen by the boss as another typical excuse. The more you talk, the less people listen.

On the other hand, when I do what needs to be done, the boss trusts that I can make things happen. The boss also knows that if I do raise an objection, it is likely to be founded on solid facts that should be considered. Since I get things done and don't constantly voice my objections, the boss actually listens. I always utilized this strategy with my senior leadership, and it worked well. I would simply make things happen as often as I could.

But how does this appear from the perspective of your subordinates? For instance, if I recognize that there are some flaws in my boss's plan, then my subordinates certainly recognize the same thing. What do I tell them? How do I preserve their respect if they think I can't see the errors the boss is making? The answer is simple—I tell them the truth. "Hey, team, I know there might be some better ways to skin this cat, but at this point, the effort to change the plan would take almost the same effort that it will to just get this job done. So we are just going to do it. And let me tell you what else we are doing by getting this done—we are building trust with the boss. Every one of these little tasks from him that we crush allows him to trust us more and more, and that gives us the ability to get listened to. So when something comes up that really doesn't make sense, he will listen. That is why we are going to execute this plan to the absolute best of our ability."

That is the truth, and the team should understand that perspective. Of course, there is a dichotomy with this. If something that makes no sense whatsoever comes down the pipe, it might be time to present some objections to the boss. If you don't, the team will recognize your failure to speak up, and you may start to appear as a pushover; you will seem like a leader who simply obeys every command from the boss without any pushback at all. This is bad not only down the chain of command but up it too. Simply being a yes-man all the time is not good. A good boss should hear, and welcome, any and all feedback or criticism of their plans. That isn't always the case, but if you have garnered clout with the boss, you can talk to them. You can present your case against their idea or plan, and they will listen. So ultimately this leads back to the beginning—one of the most powerful tools you have is a good relationship with your boss. And it doesn't end with your boss. Solid relationships up and down the chain of command are the basis of all good leadership.

PLAY THE GAME

You have to play the game. To be more specific, you have to play the long game. No one wants to hear this, especially from me. People don't want to hear about building relationships. They want me to say, "You achieve victory through blunt-force trauma. If someone gets in your way, *go through them*. Any political situation that is not turning out how you wanted can be solved with a *battle-axe!*"

That type of hyperaggressive, take-no-prisoners mentality is certainly simple and straightforward, which is often the kind of leadership advice people expect from me and what they want to hear. Because that attitude is so simple and so straightforward, it hardly seems it could fail. And often, that attitude doesn't fail—at least not at first. A heavy-handed and hostile approach usually works for a little while. You may be able to bludgeon people into doing what you want them to do for a day or two, maybe a week, maybe even a solid few months. Perhaps you can force a couple of projects to completion through ruthless and aggressive offense.

But those successes will be short lived. As you trash relationships, burn bridges, and leave scorched earth in your wake, you will soon look up and realize you are done. You have destroyed everything for short-term gain. You have nothing left.

Don't do that. Instead, you have to play the game. That means I try to support my boss and perform my duties to the best of my ability. In playing the game, I am building up trust with my boss; I am building a relationship. Why is it so important to build a good relationship with my boss? Is it so I can get promoted? Is it so I can get assigned easier tasks? No. I am not trying to build the relationship for my own personal gain; I am trying to build a relationship with my boss so we can better accomplish the mission.

And playing the game doesn't only go up the chain of command; it goes down the chain of command too. When you're the boss and your subordinates come to you objecting to something you say, listen and ask for alternatives, and when they give you a decent one, say yes to them and utilize the alternative. Even if their alternative doesn't seem quite as effective or efficient as your methodology, let them do it. This builds the trust and relationships with the people below you in the chain of command. As often as you can, listen and say yes. Eventually, when a subordinate from the team comes to you with an idea that doesn't make sense, you can say no and they won't begrudge you for it. You simply explain the issues with their idea and why you aren't going to do it that way, and they will be okay with it. They will accept your direction without feeling that you don't listen, and they will move forward with full commitment to accomplish the mission.

I always did this. I always played the game. I worked for every type of leader imaginable. Some were inspirational hands-off leaders with incredible tactical prowess. Others were micromanaging egomaniacs with no common sense. Some were paranoid, risk-averse overthinkers. But no matter what type of leader I worked for, my goal was always the same: to build a relationship with them so they trusted me, gave me what I needed to get the job done, got out of my way, and let me accomplish the mission. Building those relationships was never easy. It took doing some things that might not have been optimal. It required me swallowing my pride sometimes. It required that I play the game.

Playing the game is not easy, but it will build trust and relationships, improve the integrity of the team, and make the team more capable of accomplishing the mission. Don't let your ego or your team's ego cause turmoil. Get a grip on yourself and play the game.

Some people feel that if they play the game, if they appease their boss, if they eat crow, if they don't always drive their own personal agenda, they are weak, hypocritical sycophants. This is wrong. If you play the game, you aren't weak. You aren't kissing up to your boss. What you are doing is trying to optimize things so you and your team can best accomplish the mission. You are trying to build relationships and garner influence so you can move things in the right direction. You are not doing this for personal gain. You are not doing this for a promotion. You are playing the game so the team can win.

Can you go too far with this? Absolutely. Don't do that. Don't be a brownnoser, telling the boss that all their ideas are perfect. But be professional. Be courteous. Be genuinely interested in supporting the boss, which is another key point that people often miss. When I explain how you talk to superiors by saying things like, "Hey, boss, I just want to make sure I completely understand why you want it done this way so I can fully support your plan," I am not recommending you do this only as a way to build the relationships so you can have more influence. I am recommending it so *you actually understand why the boss wants it done a certain way.* That is real. It isn't manipulation. The goal is to *actually support your boss;* a collateral benefit is that you build the relationship, and that relationship can end up being more important than anything else.

If you are doing something small for your boss and you feel it might not be the best way, you aren't a hypocrite for following his or her instructions. You are simply storing up leadership capital for a time when it really matters. There is nothing wrong with that. It doesn't make you a hypocrite; it makes you smart.

Now, if there is something that you truly don't believe in or that you know will result in a catastrophe for the mission and the team, then it is your duty to say no. But those cases should be few and far between. So until you are asked to do something that is devastating to you, the team, and the mission, play the game and build the relationships.

WHEN IS MUTINY IN ORDER?

As important as it is to build relationships, there are times when a boss must be disobeyed. But it should be an absolute last resort. Disobeying causes massive disruption to the team, sets back progress, can fully jeopardize mission success, and may ultimately result in complete mission failure and total disintegration of the team.

But if a leader is asking the team to do something that is illegal, immoral, or unethical, it is the duty of the subordinates to refuse that order. This is obvious. It is inexcusable to do something simply because a person ordered you to do it. There is no excuse for immoral activity. If an individual is unaware of the immorality of their actions or the actions are unavoidable at a particular moment, then as soon as possible, the subordinate must report the event up the chain of command to ensure there is no further illegal activity.

There are other times when a subordinate must disobey their leader. If a leader is leading the team in a direction that will result in catastrophic failure, there is a possibility that disobeying the leader or refusing to execute orders is required. Napoleon said that if a subordinate leader executes a mission he knows is wrong, then the subordinate leader is culpable. This is the truth.

Unfortunately, few situations are that clear-cut. Again, disobeying or refusing to follow the direction of a superior is an absolute last resort because it is a final measure. Once an order has been refused, there is almost no way to unwind that action. Fortunately, there are many opportunities to avoid outright refusal or disobedience prior to the situation escalating to that point.

Before making that last stand, subordinates should ask the boss to restate the purpose of the mission, and then assess that mission statement and explain to the boss the concerns. From the boss's vantage point at a higher altitude, he or she may not see some of the granular details and understand how the plan may unfold on the front lines. It is the responsibility of the subordinate to pass this information on and to make it clear to the boss what the concerns are.

There is a chance that the boss then explains some detail that the frontline leader does not see or does not know about, which justifies the reasoning behind the boss's plan. This is a positive thing. The subordinate now understands the bigger picture and why the boss has chosen a particular course of action and can explain that to his or her team down the chain of command.

There is also a possibility that when the subordinate explains his or her concerns to the boss, the boss now sees a detail that they did not see or understand. Ideally, the subordinate not only presents the boss with his or her concerns but also presents a solution to the problem—another course of action that mitigates the subordinate's apprehension. With this revelation, the boss then reassesses the plan and either incorporates the subordinate's solution or comes up with another method of eliminating the problem.

Both of these outcomes are positive. Either the subordinate understands why the boss's plan makes sense and the subordinate agrees, or the plan is changed based on feedback from the subordinate. Either way, the plan is now considered viable by both the boss and the subordinate leaders as well as by the rest of the team once it is explained throughout the chain of command.

But that is not always the outcome. Sometimes the boss does not change their mind. Whether it is their ego or their pride or just their own inability to assess other considerations, there are times when the boss refuses to alter their plan and simply commands subordinates to move forward. When this happens, the subordinate must redouble their efforts to explain their concerns to the boss in a tactful way. Go back to the drawing board and see if there is any way to effectively implement the boss's plan without putting the mission or the team in jeopardy. Perhaps there are some smaller adjustments that can be made that still support the boss's plan but at the same time mitigate the concerns of the subordinate. If this can be done effectively, perhaps the subordinate can move forward as directed, providing the risks are not too significant. But if the risks are still a problem, take the time to go through and capture detailed potential outcomes that can be explained to the boss so they fully understand the risks involved. Then go back and present a logical, unemotional explanation of the problem.

It is important to note that in all these cases, objections to the boss should not be presented in an offensive manner. Concerns should not be presented as "This makes no sense," or "This plan is ridiculous," or "Why would we ever do this?" Statements like that are wrong on two levels. First, they come across as emotional, and when people present emotional arguments, they are not taken with the maximum degree of seriousness. Second, these statements are offensive to the person who actually came up with the plan: the boss. By attacking the boss's plan, you are attacking the boss, and in doing so, you can likely cause them to dig in and become more defensive.

It is much better to take an indirect approach. It is better for the subordinate to ask questions that put the fault on themselves. Try an approach like, "I want to make sure I understand your thinking here so I can learn to think through these issues myself," or "It's hard for me to understand this clearly since I don't have the experience you do." Each of these approaches will disarm the boss and make sure they don't feel they are under attack.

It is also a good strategy to give the boss an easy way out. If you present your own option as the only option, your leader may feel as if using someone else's plan diminishes their leadership. This is, of course, not true, but it is a perception that many people carry. So it is a powerful tool to present ideas to the boss in a way that allows them to own the plan. Perhaps offer one of the other courses of action they had mentioned, however briefly, at an earlier time. Sometimes even saying, "I was thinking about one comment you made, and it made me think that maybe we could . . ." is enough to tie an idea back to a leader so they, and their ego, feel comfortable about it. There are other ways to do this, but at a minimum, do not pit your idea against the boss's idea. That move brings out egos and can negatively impact decision-making. Instead, try to root your ideas back to the boss so the idea is tied directly to them. People almost always like their own ideas better than anyone else's.

When the boss sees a fully developed case against their plan, they are likely to either explain other details that alleviate the concerns the subordinates might not have understood or recognize the short-falls of their plan and make adjustments. Either way, the team is now aligned behind the plan.

But this is not always the case; the boss may stick to their guns and give the order to execute the plan as directed. Now the subordinate should go back again and assess the orders and plan even more granularly, looking at every possible way to mitigate risk, analyzing outcomes in even more detail, and building an even stronger case against the boss's plan. Once this is done, it is back to the boss again to present the findings.

Now, with these even more detailed and well-documented concerns presented, which still show some bad results even with the implementation of some risk mitigation, the boss will hopefully be swayed. Seeing a high potential for mission failure, presented in an inoffensive way, the boss decides on another method. This is good.

But even that doesn't always work. Sometimes a boss digs in and will not change their mind. Is it time for a mutiny? Is it time to draw a line in the sand? You could tell the boss, *"Absolutely not. I will not do this your way."* It might be the time to say that. But it also still might not be. There are many variables to assess.

First, let's observe what is at risk. Perhaps there is just a little bit of efficiency lost. If that is the case, it is not worth the fight. Maybe there is a little more substantial efficiency lost, but nothing major. If that is the case, once again, it is not worth fighting over.

But maybe there is some other, more significant risk. It may be worth going back again and really trying to explain exactly what that risk is and how it will negatively impact the mission. This idea continues—the subordinate weighing the risk involved and how impactful the final outcome will be. Eventually, the subordinate can get to a point where they are sure the outcome of the boss's plan is completely unacceptable. The subordinate knows that complying with the boss and executing as directed will have catastrophic impact on the team and the mission.

But even then, the subordinate has to contemplate if outright refusal to obey is the best call. Here are some possible outcomes when the subordinate refuses to comply:

1. The leader recognizes that the subordinate is extremely concerned about the plan—so concerned they are putting their career at stake and risking possible punitive actions—because it is actually really bad. This is the best possible outcome. The leader, awakened by the refusal of his or her subordinate to execute a plan, reconsiders the options and decides to execute a different way. Now the subordinate should rejoin the team, throw their support behind the new plan, and go help the team execute.

2. The leader digs in even deeper and will not change the plan. Since the subordinate has refused to participate, the leader fires that subordinate and puts a new subordinate in place who has been handpicked for unquestioning obedience. For the boss, the problem is solved, but the team will absolutely suffer since now the voice of reason has been replaced by one of the boss's yes-men. It will be the boss's plan, and that is it. No one will have any choice or control. This is a horrible situation. To avoid it, consider the fact that since the boss is refusing to listen to suggestions about the plan, it is probable that the boss has a big ego and is likely to put

a yes-man in to execute his or her vision without resistance. If this is a possible outcome, it must be weighed carefully.

3. If a subordinate draws a line in the sand and refuses to execute a plan or outright quits the position as a protest, they instantly remove all influence of any kind over the boss. So while the subordinate has made a very loud and clear statement, once the statement has been made, there is nothing else they can do. They are not a factor in any further outcome.

4. If the subordinate tries every possible method to convince the boss that plan is wrong and sees no way of changing the boss's mind, then perhaps the better option is for the subordinate to make one last statement of concern and then proceed to lead the team in the execution of the plan to the best of their ability. This way, the subordinate leader can at least do their utmost to mitigate the negative impacts of the poor plan, note the harmful results so they can be explained clearly to the boss, and continue to play the long game in building a relationship with the boss so they can convince the boss there is a better way to execute going forward. The inherent risk in this course of action is that, as Napoleon said, the subordinate is still culpable for the outcome.

Whatever course of action is chosen when pushing back strongly against a boss, it must be considered very carefully, since some of those courses have catastrophic outcomes for the team, the mission, and the subordinate leader. *Proceed with caution!*

BORN OR MADE?

This is an age-old question: Are leaders born or made? The answer is both.

Let's start by looking at what people are born with. Obviously, everyone is born with strengths and weaknesses in different areas. Physical attributes are obvious; some people are taller, some are shorter, some are naturally stronger, some more flexible, some are born with explosive, fast-twitch muscle and others with high-endurance, slow-twitch muscle. Physical training can certainly improve the physical capabilities of any individual. Working out with weights makes people stronger; running improves their stamina; stretching improves flexibility. But people are born with, and limited by, their own genetic makeup. These characteristics and their limitations play out clearly in sports and physical competitions. We can try to reach our genetic potential and perhaps push slightly beyond that, but eventually we are confined by our DNA.

People are also born with different cognitive capacities. Sure, with training, they can maximize their intellectual capabilities, but there will be a limit. No amount of studying can turn a person of average intelligence into Einstein. But learning, studying, and drilling can improve someone's ability to think. The more a person reads, the better they can contextualize things in the world. The more a person studies language, the better their vocabulary becomes. The more a person asks questions, practices figuring out answers, and trains their ability to think, the better they will actually be able to think. So, just as a person can improve their physical capabilities, a person can improve their intellectual competence until they reach the limits of their genomes.

The same is true with leadership characteristics. There are certain traits a human being can be born with that are beneficial for leadership.

Being articulate is one. The better a person can communicate their ideas in a simple, clear manner, the more effective a leader they will be. And some people are born more naturally articulate than others.

The ability to analyze complex problems and break them down into simple, easy-to-understand concepts is also a natural ability that some people possess, and this is a great skill for a leader to be born with. When a leader has to attack an undertaking of any kind, being able to understand the undertaking in simple terms is critical, not only so the leader can communicate to the team about the nature of the undertaking but also so the leader can identify a simple solution nested inside a sea of complexities.

The more confidence and charisma a leader has, the better he or she will do as a leader. And charisma, while hard to quantify, is an identifiable trait that human beings have—and they have different amounts. Some people have an incredible amount of natural magnetism, and others are drawn to them. Some might struggle even to get a minuscule level of attention paid to them.

Even a trait like being loud is a good leadership quality to have. If you are going to lead, people need to hear you, but if your voice is not loud, the team will not be able to hear your directions and therefore will not be able to execute.

The ability to read people is very important, but it, too, doesn't come naturally to everyone. In fact, some people do a horrible job of interacting with others. They are socially awkward and don't pick up on other people's emotions and reactions.

All leaders have strengths and weaknesses. Fortunately, they can improve. How?

First, a leader can become more articulate. They can practice speaking, study to expand their vocabulary, and read and write to practice and improve their ability to clarify and communicate their thoughts. In doing these things, they become more articulate over time.

A leader can also get better at simplifying things. By detaching and thinking about problems more abstractly, by making simplification their goal, and by continually reprioritizing or removing things that are not really important, over time and with practice the leader will improve their ability to develop simpler solutions.

Charisma might be hard for a leader to improve, but they can certainly make some progress. The leader can pay attention to their posture and countenance. As the leader gains experience, they also gain confidence, which helps their charisma. A leader can also focus on things like looking people in the eye when talking to them, listening intently to what others say, and speaking clearly with humble authority. The leader can make sure they project their voice so they are heard. All those little things add up to increased charisma.

To improve their ability to read people, the leader can start to pay more attention to body language, facial expressions, and tone of voice. Once the leader is paying attention, they can figure out what a person's baseline of behavior is and then begin to identify when the person deviates from that baseline, which will help indicate the person's feelings or mood.

So there are quantifiable ways for leaders to improve their natural leadership characteristics, but it would be unrealistic to think a leader can go from a low level in any category to an exceptional level, just as it would be unrealistic to turn a world champion marathon runner into an Olympic champion weight lifter. The genes just aren't there.

So how can a leader become great if they lack the natural characteristics necessary to lead? The answer is simple: a good leader builds a great team that counterbalances their weaknesses.

I saw this take place when I was running tactical training for the SEAL Teams. There was a task unit commander in charge of two SEAL platoons who didn't have a loud voice. He was smart and tactically savvy, and he seemed to be respected by his troops, but he had the vocal cords of a mouse. While it is certainly a benefit for any leader to be able to project their voice, it is absolutely critical for a combat leader to be able to make themselves heard. The reason is obvious: during a machine-gun fight, it gets extremely loud. And yet direction still has to be given in a loud and thunderous tone so the rest of the team can hear the call and then pass it on.

Unfortunately, this was beyond the capability of this particular SEAL officer. I counseled him about it directly. "Your men can't hear you. You need to get louder."

"I'm not sure I can," he told me.

"Well, you'd better, because right now, your weak voice is rendering you ineffective as a leader," I replied, being as blunt as I could to try to get him to remedy the situation.

I watched and listened to him during the next training exercise. There was no improvement. His team lagged behind because they could not hear his orders.

After that training mission, I addressed it again with the officer. During the next mission, there was still no improvement.

I started to wonder if this individual could actually be effective as a SEAL leader, and my suspicions drifted toward no. I was born with a naturally loud voice, and that voice had always served me well as a SEAL leader. I reflected on the times when my loud voice was able to pierce through the noise of the gunfire and explosions and be heard by my men. It was a critical capability. You might think the radios we use with the high-tech, noise-canceling headsets would solve this problem, but it doesn't. During the chaos of a gunfight, people often can't hear their radios, and even if they can, they can't always pay attention to them. Commands are lost in the mayhem.

But verbal commands are different. Every SEAL is trained since day one of the basic SEAL training course to stop shooting when they hear a command being yelled, look at the person who just yelled the command, repeat the command back to them, then look at the person next to them in the opposite direction, pass the word on to them, and then wait for them to yell it back, ensuring they got the word. This does not happen when commands are passed on the radio; that is why commands and directions are so often lost on the radio.

I really started to question the potential of the quiet SEAL officer and further addressed it with him. "Look. I see that you understand tactics. I see that you are good at planning. I even see that you are making good tactical decisions. But none of that matters if your men can't hear you. You need to get louder, and you need to get louder now, or else you aren't going to make it."

He was disappointed by my words, but not angry. I think he truly recognized his shortcoming and how badly it was impacting his entire task unit.

Soon, it was time for the next training mission to take place. Once again, I kept my eye on the quiet, young task unit commander. As the mission unfolded, so did the chaos, the mayhem, and the noise. Automatic weapons were ripping off thousands of rounds of belt-fed blanks. Simulated artillery grenades were whining and exploding. It became very hard to hear, but a call needed to be made. The team needed to enter, clear a building, and set security, a maneuver we call *strongpoint*. It was the obvious decision.

I eyed the task unit commander. He looked like he knew what to do, but could he bark loudly enough to make everyone hear him so they could execute? Just as I started to wonder, I watched him tell one of his guys, whom I'll call Bill, "Tell everyone to strongpoint that building right there and set security!"

I saw the task unit commander's brilliance immediately; Bill was the loudest bigmouth in the entire task unit. As soon as he heard the order from his boss, Bill thundered out, "All right, everyone—strongpoint that building right there and set security!"

Just as they had been trained, when people heard that call, they passed the word to the next SEAL and then to the next. Soon all the task unit members had not only heard the call, they were actually executing it, taking down the building and setting security. It was awesome to watch. It proved verbal commands worked. But it also proved that I was wrong.

The SEAL officer was absolutely capable of leading men in combat. He just needed to figure out how to utilize the people on his team to cover for his weaknesses.

And that is what a good leader does—finds other people to bring onto the team who compensate for his or her shortfalls. By doing that, even the biggest deficits in leadership traits can be overcome. Combine that with hard work to try to improve on areas of weakness, and soon any person can drastically improve their ability to lead.

Well, I should say *almost* anyone. Because there is one type of person who can never become a good leader: a person who lacks humility. People who lack humility cannot improve because they don't acknowledge their own weaknesses. They don't work to improve them, and they won't bring someone onto the team to offset their shortfalls. This person will never improve. Beware.

But everyone else can get better. And while you might not be able to transform an awful leader into an excellent one, you can certainly make a bad leader a better one and a good leader an outstanding one, regardless of how they were born.

LEADERSHIP AND MANIPULATION

Leadership and manipulation are closely related, but one is deemed to be bad and the other is considered good. They are closely related because they are both trying to do the same thing: the aim of both leadership and manipulation is to get people to do what you want them to do. The highest form of both leadership and manipulation is to get people to do what you want them to do because *they want* to do it.

Both leaders and manipulators use many of the same techniques. They both build relationships, leverage their influence, and maneuver politically to attain the outcome they desire. Both leaders and manipulators capitalize on others' egos, personal agendas, and individual strengths and weaknesses to achieve their own preferred outcome.

But while there are many similarities between leaders and manipulators, there is one glaring difference: manipulators are trying to get people to do things that will benefit the manipulator, while leaders are trying to get people to do things that will benefit the team and the people themselves. This difference is stark. The manipulator is trying to get a promotion or a better position for themselves. The manipulator is trying to set themselves up to look good in the eyes of their boss. The manipulator has one ultimate priority in every move they make: that priority is the manipulator.

But a leader puts themselves at the bottom of the priority list. The good of the mission and the good of the team outweigh any personal concern a true leader has for themselves.

Both of these attitudes eventually shine through and reveal themselves. Manipulators might fool some of the people some of the time, but they won't fool all the people all the time. True leaders are the same; while they might not always get the credit they deserve because they deflect it to other team members, over time they will absolutely be recognized, admired—and likely promoted—for their leadership.

This does not mean the leader always triumphs over the manipulator in the immediate situation. Sometimes a manipulator plays a good hand, gets himself or herself noticed, and winds up winning. But the win will be short term. Sacrificing others for yourself never pans out in the long term; people eventually notice and take stock of the fact that you are not looking out for the good of the team, but instead you are looking out for yourself. When people notice that, they will not follow you for long.

The same thing happens to a good leader; their true goals are eventually revealed. When a good leader makes sacrifices and puts other people and the mission ahead of themselves, eventually that will be recognized and people will want to follow that leader. Good leaders do the right things for the right reasons; they work hard, support the team, and lead solid execution. In the long run, the reputation of a true leader far outweighs the glory-seeking manipulator, and in the end, the good leader, looking out for the mission and the team, will win.

SUBORDINATE YOUR EGO

At Echelon Front, our leadership consultancy, Leif and I began working with a company that was growing quickly and making a lot of money. They recognized that they needed to get ahead of the growth by training junior leaders to be ready to step up and take greater responsibility.

This initial trip was to be an assessment, where Leif and I would interview people at every level of leadership, learn more about their business, and start to develop a plan to train the junior leaders.

The first day, we met with the senior executives from the company. I was very impressed with them all. The COO was smart and capable. The CFO was out of central casting, astute and detail-oriented. The CTO, the HR lead, and the rest of the senior executive leaders were all solid.

Then I met the CEO. I had done my research, and on paper he appeared to be the best of the best. He was an NCAA college athlete. He went to an Ivy League school for his MBA. And he was young, not even in his midthirties yet, but was already running a hundred-million-dollar company.

He was also physically impressive; he was at least six foot five and had to be a solid 250 pounds of muscle.

But it wasn't only his physical size that was big; as soon as we shook hands, I realized his ego was also massive. The look on his face screamed, *I'm better than you are!* and I could almost feel him bowing out his chest like a teenage boy trying to act tough.

I felt an immediate tension from him—borderline smugness as he looked down his nose at me.

No big deal, I thought as I looked at him. I had dealt with many big egos both in the military and in the corporate world.

But I soon realized that this case would be particularly challenging. Every comment he made was haughty and arrogant. Anything I said was greeted with a superior look of *I already knew that.* I thought he would open up to some of my ideas as the day went on, but he didn't; his conceit and condescension hit me like a baseball bat with almost every word he spoke.

We finished out the day with the senior executives, and the next day we met some of the midlevel managers and frontline leaders. I dug around a little bit as we talked to them, looking for some dirt on the CEO—to see what they thought of his overly prideful attitude. But none of them made any statements against him; in fact, most said they liked him and respected him. *He's got all of them fooled,* I thought.

Once we wrapped that up, we departed the company and began

to formulate our plan for the next steps. As I thought about the discrepancy between the CEO's attitude and his team's assessment of him, I began to think he was probably just having a bad day when we met. Perhaps something had made him mad—a missed deadline or a failing project, and that anger just seeped over into his attitude toward me. *That had to have been the case,* I thought. Especially because I pride myself on being able to get along with anyone, and I certainly couldn't see why he had any legitimate reason to treat me with such an egotistical attitude. I figured the next time we went out to work with him, he would step down from his high horse and treat me with respect.

I was wrong. Again, everything was great with the rest of the senior leaders when we showed up to begin the leadership training for the team. They were happy to see us and excited to start the program.

Except him. Even when we shook hands, I could feel his conceited self-importance. *What in the hell is wrong with this guy?* I wondered. As I kicked off the first training session, his attitude didn't budge. As I explained leadership principles, he listened, but at the same time he tried not to seem too interested. He looked at his phone, whispered to a few people. Even got up and walked out for a few minutes as if everything he was doing was infinitely more important than the leadership lessons I was teaching. When I was done with the first session, Leif took over the second session. I sat there looking at this egomaniacal jerk wondering how he ended up that way and why he couldn't see how much of a pompous blowhard he was. I tried to figure out how to handle this problem *he* had. How could *he* be so egotistical? How could *he* not see his own arrogance?

Then I thought a little deeper. How was it that his fellow executives didn't seem bothered by his ego? How was it that his frontline leaders didn't see the same conceit and self-importance that I saw?

Wait, I thought. *Is it possible the problem is me?*

It hit me like a bolt of lightning. Could it be my ego causing this problem? Was there a chance that my fragile self-image could be threatened by this beast of a human being, who was not only physically gifted in size, strength, and athletic ability but also was extremely smart, a bold leader, and was running a hundred-million-dollar company—all at the age of thirty-two? Was there a chance that my ego was intimidated by all this and that I was the one who was acting like an idiot?

Of course. Now that I saw what was happening, it was obvious—our two massive egos were bumping into each other and causing friction.

During the next break, I approached him and said, "Hey, can I talk to you for a minute outside?"

He gave me a smirk and then sneered, "Sure . . . you gonna give me some *coaching*?" with the utter contempt in his voice when he said the word *coaching*.

I motioned outside with my head and walked toward the door of the classroom. He followed me. We walked down the hallway to get out of earshot of the rest of the team. I stopped, turned around, and studied his face; he looked like I had just asked him to step outside for a fight.

"Well?" he finally said.

I smiled. "Well," I replied, "I just wanted to give you a quick assessment of everything I've seen so far. Your leaders are solid. Your company has great morale, and they really understand the mission here." His face changed slightly. He looked a little disarmed. This was not what he was expecting.

"But the most impressive thing I have seen here so far," I continued, "is *you*. You are smart; you have great presence. Everyone here really understands your vision. It is obvious that everything great I see at this company is a reflection of your leadership, which is outstanding. And it is no surprise. You played ball in college, you have the Ivy League education, you stay in great shape, and you've built this powerful company. It is impressive, to say the least. I have nothing but respect for you, what you have done, and what you are going to do."

By the time I finished that last sentence, his face had completely changed. The arrogance disappeared and was replaced with a humble, almost bashful face.

"No way!" he blurted out. "I'm just a business guy. You are the one who deserves respect! You spent your whole life in the SEAL Teams! You rose up through the ranks! You led men in combat in an incredibly hard environment. That is what deserves respect!"

We both laughed as the tension between our egos disappeared. Our relationship turned 180 degrees in a matter of seconds. We walked back to the classroom, and he was fully engaged in everything I said about business, leadership, and life. He even began chiming in and relating his own experiences to support the principles I was touting.

The problem was solved. How had I done it? Simple. As soon as I was able to detach and recognize that this was a clash of egos, all I had to do was humble myself for a minute; I had to subordinate my own ego to allow the tension to break. Once I did that, the problem was solved.

Ego is like reactive armor; the harder you push against it, the more it pushes back. If I had confronted the CEO about his attitude and told him he had a big ego, he would have dug in even deeper. So I did the opposite. I disarmed his ego by subduing my own.

You might be afraid that if you subordinate your ego, you will get trampled. But that normally doesn't happen because subordinating your ego is actually the ultimate form of self-confidence. That level of confidence earns respect. So while the initial thought or feeling might be that you backed down, you have actually shown you have the strength and confidence to give the other person credit, and they will recognize and respect that confidence, either consciously or subconsciously.

And that is the truth. To put your ego in check, to subordinate your ego, you must have incredible confidence. If you find you cannot put your ego in check because you are afraid it might make you look weak, then guess what? You *are* weak. Don't be weak.

Subordinate your ego, build relationships, and win the long game.

LEADERS TELL THE TRUTH

Truth and honesty are perhaps the most essential of leadership qualities. Tell the truth to your people. Tell the truth to your boss. Tell the truth to your peers. And, of course, tell the truth to yourself.

This is no easy task. And telling the truth does not give a leader, subordinate, or peer the right to be a jerk or to attack people. No. Telling the truth must be done with tact and sensitivity.

Of course, some truths are easy to speak: "We are winning!" "You are doing an amazing job." "Our competitors don't stand a chance." Who wouldn't want to speak these truths?

But there are harder truths that are more difficult to tell: "We are losing." "Your performance is substandard." "The enemy is gaining ground on us." Those truths hurt as much to say as they do to hear. That is why so many people, especially leaders, fail to deliver the hard truth.

But leaders must speak the truth.

To do that, a leader must first know his or her people and communicate often with them. That way, if a leader has bad news to tell the team members, it isn't the first time he or she is speaking to them. Delivering bad news shouldn't be the one time in the last four months the leader has come down to the front lines to speak to the troops. No. There should be a consistent, well-established relationship with the troops so they know and understand the leader and the leader knows and understands the troops. The more communication there is with subordinates, the easier it should be to communicate with them, even if the things being communicated are negative. Additionally, when there is a solid relationship, it allows the subordinates to deliver bad news—to speak the truth—up the chain of command too.

If you communicate often—and by *communicate* I mean all forms of communication, including meetings, phone calls, emails, texts, videos, and any other method available—then the bad news will sting less. For instance, let's say a company loses a 5 percent market share one month, and the CEO does not share that with anyone in hopes that they gain the market share back. If they do gain the market share back, then all is good. But if they lose another 5 percent market share—now totaling 10 percent market share—that is much harder to explain. So hard, in fact, that some bosses might not want to share it. Instead, they cross their fingers and hope to recover the next month. Once again, if the company begins to recover market share and stays on a positive trajectory, perhaps everything will turn out all right. But if they don't, the CEO can look up in three months or six months or a year with 50 percent of their market share *gone*. Then what? Now telling the truth becomes very hard, because the truth is, the company has lost 50 percent of its market share and is going to have to cut marketing, training, and personnel to survive. Not good.

But if the CEO had told the truth earlier, and done it in a positive way, things could very well have been different. If he or she had told the troops that market share had gone down 5 percent, the troops could have realized that they needed to push a little harder. The frontline personnel and leaders could have redoubled their efforts and done more to make things happen. They could have recovered market share and put the company on a new path to success. But failing to tell the truth, early and often, makes that type of recovery impossible.

On top of that, the troops will find out when the truth isn't told. They will see declining numbers. Someone in accounting will tell someone in operations or sales about declining revenue. That bit of reality injected into the void of information on the front lines will result in rumors about the impending catastrophe. This rumor mill will compound and eventually become a self-fulfilling prophecy of doom. This is gossip and groupthink; if the frontline troops aren't sure why something is happening, they will make up their own reasons, and the reasons they come up with will likely be much worse than reality. *Why would the boss hide the truth unless it was a total disaster?*

How do you combat that vicious cycle? Kill the rumors by telling the truth.

Perhaps the worst result of a leader not telling the team members the truth is that they simply will not trust the leader anymore. They will not believe what the leader says, they will not believe in the leader's plan, and they will not believe in the leader's vision. When the team members do not believe in the leader's words, plan, or vision, the team and the leader will fail.

Despite this, there are still many occasions where people don't tell the truth. Sometimes they think there is a legitimate reason not to tell the truth. In the military, perhaps some information is compartmentalized, classified material. In the civilian sector, maybe legal action forbids the sharing of certain information.

When those situations occur, the answer is simple: tell the truth. Not the truth that is classified and therefore illegal to reveal but the truth about why the truth can't be told.

"I'm sorry, but that is actually classified and compartmentalized information that I am not allowed to discuss."

Or: "Listen, I would like to share that information with you, but due to the legal situation, I cannot disclose it right now."

A leader also has to tell the truth when a mistake is made, which is inherent in taking Extreme Ownership of it. The owner must tell the truth about what happened, what went wrong, what mistakes they made, and how they are going to fix them.

But telling the truth does not mean a leader cannot use the truth as an excuse to be overly critical or offensive. This is most easily mitigated by having a relationship with and caring about the members of the team. Know who they are. Know what they stand for. Know what drives them. If a leader lacks that knowledge, he or she will not be able to communicate effectively with the team, especially when it comes to delivering critique points or harsh truths.

If you have a harsh truth to deliver to the team, it is best to just deliver it. Of course, explain the circumstances around it, but don't make any excuses or hold anything back. Just tell the truth and explain why. Have to terminate some people? Explain why that is necessary for the good of the team. Need to put in some extra hours that no one wants to? Explain the reason why it is important. And then lead from the front, especially when things are bad. You take the pay cut. You take the first shift of the overtime work. As a leader, do the hard things. Don't leave it to the troops.

The same is true when it comes to communicating with individuals. Don't wait to have hard conversations; they will only get harder. Whether it is a subordinate, a superior, a peer, or a client, waiting to discuss a difficult issue will not make the issue any less difficult. Attack it.

But remember, even with hard truths in the form of individual criticism, truth is not an excuse to show bad tact; in fact, hard truths require more tact. If you have a good relationship with your subordinate, and they know you care about them, hard truths should be similar to the natural conversations you already have.

One common technique that gets discussed is to sandwich negative criticism between two positive points. "Your team has hit their numbers three months straight, which is great to see. But your churn rate with employees is not good; you are losing too many people. This is offset by the fact that they are definitely performing well while they are here."

This technique is an attempt to build a shortcut around having actual relationships with your direct reports. You shouldn't have to manufacture good points to wrap around bad points. If a leader has a good relationship with his or her subordinates, this won't be necessary.

That being said, a good relationship with subordinates does not mean the subordinate is magically open to harsh criticism. It doesn't work that way. The vast majority of the population doesn't like criticism no matter who it comes from, so most criticism is best delivered indirectly, with the minimal amount of negativity needed to get the desired change. (See how to deliver criticism on page 271.)

STUDY

Leaders are never good enough. A leader must be constantly improving and learning since, in any leadership job, new and unexpected challenges arise all the time and, as one continues to lead, the number of people being led increases, projects multiply in number and scope, and the overall strategic impact of the missions being led also expands.

Leadership in any chosen profession is just that—a profession. Being a leader is your life. Do everything humanly possible to know and understand everything there is about your profession and being a leader in that profession. Strive every day to learn and become a better leader.

There are many components for learning to lead. One of the most important is to try to see everything through the lens of leadership.

In any group of people, leadership is occurring. Pay attention to that. Observe what works and what doesn't. Note the successful and unsuccessful techniques leaders use—how they talk, words they use, interactions they carry out. Think about how you can apply these techniques.

Apply the leadership lens to things you read. Almost every story has a component of leadership embedded in it; a book or article does not have to be about leadership to be *about leadership*. Pay attention to that. How does the leader act? What does the leader say? How do the leader's superiors and subordinates react? Learning from history through books is a great way to gain experience without having to live through it, but this only works if you can read with the correct level of engagement to understand the actions, emotions, and human nature inside the words themselves.

Also, learn to pay attention to the small things. We often overlook the nuances of situations and then wonder why things unfolded the way they did. Pay attention. Little things matter; they matter less, but they matter.

Think about the fundamental principles of leadership and overlay them onto everything you see to expand your thinking. Cover and Move. Simple. Prioritize and Execute. Decentralized Command. Extreme Ownership. The Dichotomy of Leadership. If you look for these principles, you will see them; if you see them, you will understand them better. The better you understand them, the better you can implement them; the better you can implement them, the more you can look for them, and this cycle continues forever.

None of this happens without humility. If a leader thinks they have achieved the pinnacle of leadership expertise, they are already going in the wrong direction, stagnant in their skill set, and, worst of all, unconsciously giving off the stink of arrogance. Don't let this happen. Stay humble, and always learn.

CORE TENETS

BE CAPABLE AND ASK FOR HELP

A leader must know and understand the jobs, skills, and equipment used by the people below him or her in the chain of command. This isn't to say a leader needs to be an expert in everything; that is impossible. A platoon commander does not know as much about shooting as his snipers do. He can't understand the various radios as well as his radioman does. He will not know the details of routes to and from a target like the point man will. On a construction site, the foreman won't be able to operate equipment with the same efficiency as those who operate that equipment all day long. He won't be able to lay block as well as the masons or tie rebar like an ironworker. In the manufacturing business, a plant manager might not able to run each machine or handle every task on the line. But in all these cases, the leader must at least be familiar with what goes on below him in the chain of command.

What should a leader do if he doesn't know or understand a skill or a job that plays a role in the accomplishment of the mission? Simple: ask. That's right. Go and ask—and not just for an explanation; ask to learn and actually do. Sight in that sniper weapon. Program that radio. Lay some block. Run that piece of equipment for a little while. Get familiar and then actually practice the task.

Unfortunately, most people avoid this process because they fear they will look stupid. They think their subordinates will lose respect for them. But the opposite is true. This is another area where ego can be a real impediment to success. Some leaders feel it is a weakness to ask for help. That couldn't be further from the truth. Subordinates will actually respect the leader more if they come and try to learn and perform the task. What subordinates don't respect is a leader who tries to appear to know everything. I know this from experience. When I was a junior-ranking SEAL, I was always impressed by a boss who would come and truly show interest in what we were doing on the front lines. I was even more impressed if they asked questions and wanted to really understand my perspective. And I would be completely impressed if the leader physically tried to do what I was doing—program a radio, shoot an advanced weapons system, or build a demolition charge. If you need help with something, ask for it. Subordinates understand that their leaders might not know everything. Put your ego in check, and ask for help. You will do a better job, and you will gain respect from your team. Stepping down and learning frontline skills also shows your humility. It proves you aren't above what the frontline troops are doing, and it shows you know their job is hard.

But remember, being a leader who is not required to be able to perform tasks assigned to the front lines is not an excuse for being ignorant or unprepared. If you are going down to the front lines, at least be familiar with what those on the front lines do. Look at the manuals so you are aware of the equipment they are using. Study what you can so you don't look completely lost. This goes for leaders at every level. It is understandable that a leader might not know exactly how to operate a piece of gear or equipment, but it is inexcusable not to know what it is or at least what it is used for. Complete ignorance of what is happening on the front lines makes you appear out of touch, and, yes, the troops will lose respect for you. If that happens and you are caught unprepared, step away, dive in, and learn what you can. Then come back for more.

And speaking of coming back for more, just because you have gone down and done something once doesn't mean you are good to go. Always go back for more. Keep learning and getting better. I told the CEO of an equipment manufacturer that he should go and build a product from beginning to end at least once a month so he was always in touch with the process; that way, he would understand the challenges his frontline workers experienced firsthand. It also meant he had the knowledge to call someone out if they were trying to pull the wool over his eyes. That is worth its weight in gold.

Lastly, when you get down in the dirt with the frontline troops, you get to know them. You build relationships. And when you have relationships with the frontline troops, they actually tell you what is going on. They give you information. They tell you what is working and what isn't. That is powerful knowledge to have. Of course, you can't spend all your time with the frontline troops; you have to balance that.

But make sure you do spend enough time with them, and make sure you know what they do. Get down with the frontline troops, learn what you can from them, know and understand their part of the mission, and earn their respect as a leader and as a person.

BUILDING TRUST
AND RELATIONSHIPS

Relationships up and down the chain of command are the foundation of a team. If two people trust each other, they have a relationship; if there is no trust, there is no relationship. So relationships are built on trust. Teams are built on relationships. If there aren't relationships between people, there is no team, just a group of random people.

We need to build relationships to form a team, and we need to build trust to build relationships. So the question is: How can we build trust, relationships, and, in the end, our team?

The most obvious part of building trust, and thereby building a relationship, is honesty (covered in "Leaders Tell the Truth," page 78). But while telling the truth is the foundation, there are other tools to help build trust. Here are some strategic methods to build trust up and down.

DOWN THE CHAIN

To build trust and relationships down the chain of command, you have to *give* trust. What does that mean? If I want my subordinates to trust me, I need to give them trust. So, for instance, I will allow—and trust—them to run a mission. I will allow—and trust—them to make a decision. I will allow—and trust—them to work through a problem without my oversight.

Of course, there is inherent risk when I allow my subordinates to run a mission, make a decision, or work through a problem. The risk is that they might make a bad decision, fail to solve a problem, or fail the mission. That is why, as a leader, I will start to build trust with small, incremental steps. The first mission I trust a subordinate to run will not be a major, real-world operation with strategic consequences; instead, it will be a simple training operation with nothing at stake but ego and pride. I would not allow a decision to be made that might have significant negative impact if my subordinate makes the wrong call; instead, I would select a decision for the subordinate to make that would cause little trouble if the wrong decision were made. It is the same for allowing a subordinate to solve a problem. I wouldn't give them a problem to solve where failure to solve the problem would result in a broader catastrophe; instead, I would give the subordinate a problem that would be easy to recover from should a solution not be found in a timely manner.

In each case, if my subordinate were successful, my trust would increase. Also, since I gave the subordinate leeway to make the decision, their trust in me would increase. They would begin to trust that I gave good guidance, trust that I allowed them room to work without micromanaging them, and trust that I would let them solve problems and figure things out for themselves. When one of my subordinates was successful in these tasks, I would begin looking for a slightly bigger mission for them to run, a little bigger decision for them to make, and an even bigger problem for them to solve. This process would repeat over and over again, gradually and incrementally increasing the trust between us.

If a subordinate failed in carrying out a mission or making the right decision or solving a problem, I wouldn't drop the hammer of punishment on them. I wouldn't berate or belittle them. Instead, I would look at their mistake as an opportunity to teach them, to counsel them, to mentor them. If I thought they understood, I would give them another mission, decision, or problem to deal with. Perhaps I would give them just a little more guidance and oversight this time to make sure they did a better job. Once they were successful, I would follow the same procedure above, gradually increasing the size and magnitude of the mission, decision, or problem, continuing to increase the trust between us.

As time goes on, the missions, decisions, and problems become more difficult, and the subordinates will make mistakes. Again, these are simply learning opportunities that make the subordinate better. As the risk in the situations escalates, you can still let them lead, but just provide more oversight to make sure they don't make a mistake that could cause an unacceptable loss; you micromanage them a little bit. You make corrections for them as they get slightly off track to ensure there isn't a catastrophic failure, and yet they still learn from those little adjustments.

What starts out as micromanagement becomes more and more hands-off. The more trust that is built, the more hands-off the leader can be. Eventually, the subordinate will have successfully carried out enough missions, decisions, and problem solving and learned enough along the way that full trust is achieved.

UP THE CHAIN

We also have to develop trust and build relationships with our superiors. Once again, the process starts with telling the truth. The mistake that often gets made here is that subordinates like to tell their bosses what *they think their bosses want to hear.* Whether it is telling the boss "Morale is great with the troops" when it isn't or "We are heading in the right direction and will definitely make our sales numbers" or even "We have all the support we need," these assertions can cause problems if they aren't the truth. All these statements might make the boss feel good in the short term, but in the long term they are going to come back and hurt the mission, the team, and, ultimately, the boss. When it comes back and hurts the boss, the boss will remember it was you who fed them incorrect information, and their trust in you will obviously be diminished.

So you have to tell the truth. But remember, this does not give you permission to complain. The truth might be that your team has been working hard and a break would be nice. That isn't worth telling the boss, who likely doesn't need to hear that. But if the team members are extremely fatigued and truly need some rest before they make a significant mistake, that *is* worth telling the boss. Make sure you distinguish between telling the truth about things the boss needs to know and complaining about every little thing that goes on.

As mentioned in earlier sections, a couple of other things that are important in building trust are simply performing well and being tactful when you push back against the boss.

All these strategies must be employed to build trust. Without trust, leadership falls apart.

TRUST AND DECENTRALIZED COMMAND

One of the most critical requirements for trust is the use of Decentralized Command. Trust must be well established because there are times when the only thing holding a team together up and down the chain of command is trust. There are dynamic situations when there is not time for a leader to explain why he or she needs the job done. Instead, the leader just needs the subordinate to execute immediately.

This always seems contrary to everything I teach, not only about Decentralized Command but about leadership in general. Over and over again, I tell people not to bark orders, not to impose plans on subordinates, and to make sure everyone understands not just what you want them to do but, more important, *why* they need to do it. Once they understand *why* they are doing what they are doing, they can take ownership and carry out the task with the knowledge and clarity to make adjustments as needed.

On top of that, I also always encourage questions from subordinates; if they don't understand *why* they are doing something, they need to ask. If subordinates disagree with a plan or idea, they need to raise their concerns up the chain of command. This kind of resistance to and pushback against the boss will create a better result in the end. After all, the leader has a different view of the situation from that of the troops on the front line, so the leader might not see what the subordinates see. A leader can easily make a bad decision because of their lack of perspective. Therefore, it is essential that there be open dialogue between subordinates and the leader so the situation can be understood and different perspectives can be seen up and down the chain of command. With open dialogue, the best possible plan can be formulated.

But what about a time-sensitive situation in which a decision must be made quickly? Let's say I am a SEAL platoon commander in an urban combat situation and my platoon is attacked with heavy machine-gun fire while crossing a road. Several of my platoon members are pinned down behind some of the vehicles in the street. I assess the situation and quickly determine that we need to put down suppressive fire from an elevated position, which will allow the pinned-down platoon members to maneuver out of the street. I analyze the layout of the platoon and recognize squad two is in the best position to make it happen, so I look at the second squad leader—we'll call him Fred—and bark, "Fred, get your squad to that building on the corner, get to the roof, and start putting down suppressive fire!"

At this point, Fred doesn't say, "Well, you know, boss, can you give me some background as to *why* you want that done? I'm thinking there are some other possible solutions to this problem that we should explore." That would be ridiculous. He knows the situation is critical. He knows this is no time to debate. And most important, he trusts me. We have been working together for months. I have made plenty of decisions that he questioned, and when he did question them, I was open to his questions, and we came to conclusions that we both agreed on. Fred knows that I always want him to understand *why* he is doing what he is doing. I was always more than willing to take the time to explain and discuss the *why* in great detail whenever I could.

But Fred also knows now isn't the time for discussion, explanation, or a question-and-answer session. Now is the time for action. Now is the time for trust. So Fred yells back "Got it!" and goes into action and executes the plan.

That is the way it works.

But it doesn't work that way every time, because there is a chance that when I bark an order at Fred, he will look back at me and yell, "*Negative!*"

That's right, my subordinate, who knows me and trusts me and knows that we are in a critical situation, might look back at me and scream, "Negative!" He isn't going to do what I need him to do. Why is that? Has he lost his confidence and trust in me? Does he feel he doesn't need to listen? No. The answer is simple: Fred sees something that I don't see. Perhaps he sees an enemy improvised explosive device outside the building; maybe he sees enemy personnel that I can't see. It could be any number of things, but for some reason Fred realizes he cannot carry out my order.

This is once again where trust plays a huge role in an effective team. Not only did *he* have to trust *me* when I first gave him the order to go to the building, but now that he has said "Negative" to me, *I* have to trust *him*. I have to trust that he's seen something that I don't see; I have to trust that he would do everything to carry out my order if he could—but he can't.

Now I have to adjust. Instead of telling him what to do, I actually take a step back and tell him *why* I need him to do it. "We need cover fire from an elevated position so we can maneuver!"

At this point, Fred knows why I need what I need, so he comes up with a way to make it happen. He sees a building adjacent to the one I wanted him to take and points to it, shouting, "Roger that! I'm moving my squad to that building there, and we'll get on the roof to provide cover fire!"

"*Go!*" I reply.

With that, he executes.

He was able to execute—*we* were able to execute—not only because of Decentralized Command and his understanding of the *why* but also because of the relationships we had built, through trust, up and down the chain of command. That is leadership.

EARNING INFLUENCE AND RESPECT

Just as a leader must build trust and relationships up and down the chain of command, a leader must also earn influence and respect. Too often, leaders think they *deserve* to be respected because of their rank or experience. Similarly, they think their position of authority equates to influence. And they are right to an extent. When a leader is in a position of senior rank, there is some respect and influence that is inherent in that rank. Generally, a subordinate looks to a superior and expects that their superior's training and experience will give the superior the ability to make good decisions and lead the team in the right direction. Rank and position do carry some level of respect and influence.

But such respect and influence are extremely limited. The leader needs to build upon that initial platform and increase the respect and influence they receive from the troops as much as possible. How is that done? Similar to building trust, to build respect and influence you have to give respect and influence.

Treat people with respect. What does that mean? Allow them to give their opinion. Listen to them. Don't interrupt them. Don't disparage the importance of their job or position. Share the burden of hard tasks.

The same is true for influence. If you want to have influence over others, you need to allow them to have influence over you. That means when you listen to them, you actually *listen*. You consider their recommendations and, whenever possible, you incorporate their thoughts and ideas into whatever you are trying to accomplish. You keep an open mind.

The more you respect people and allow people to influence you, the more respect you will gain, and the more influence you will have over them.

EXTREME OWNERSHIP OF EVERYTHING

One of the most important tenets of leadership I adhered to as a leader in my military career was the idea of Extreme Ownership. It meant that when something went wrong, as the leader it was my fault. If there was a failure of some kind up or down the chain of command, then I was responsible for it. I wrote about this in the first chapter of my first book, *Extreme Ownership.*

The idea of Extreme Ownership has struck a chord with people, and it has been incredibly effective in helping those in all kinds of leadership positions leading all kinds of teams in all kinds of industries, businesses, and professions. Leaders found that when they took ownership of everything in their world, they saw other members of their teams, both up and down the chain of command, taking ownership as well. When people take ownership of their jobs and their mission, the jobs get done and the mission gets accomplished. When there are problems and people take ownership of those problems, the problems get solved.

While Extreme Ownership might seem like a fairly simple concept to understand, it can be difficult to fully comprehend what it *really means.* What it *really means* is that the leader is responsible for everything. *Absolutely everything.*

This can be hard to fully understand because there are times when a subordinate does something that the boss feels they cannot control and cannot possibly be responsible for. A subordinate might make a mistake or take an action that is completely unexpected. How can that be the leader's fault?

I like to use the example of a young machine gunner in a SEAL platoon to exemplify how a leader truly is responsible for everything that happens. A SEAL machine gunner plays a key role in a SEAL platoon. As the name implies, he carries a machine gun—a heavy, belt-fed weapon capable of firing over seven hundred rounds per minute. The machine gun's ability to lay down such massive firepower makes it critical to a SEAL platoon or squad because it is the main weapon that puts down suppressive fire on the enemy; it keeps the enemy's heads down, allowing the rest of the SEALs to maneuver. The machine gun provides the main source of cover in the fundamental tactic of Cover and Move—the first law of combat.

Of course, the machine gun doesn't operate itself; it is worthless without the machine gunner. The machine gunner carries the weapon and its ammunition, maintains the weapon, loads and fires the weapon. Those are the mechanics of his job. But a machine gunner must also be aware of how to best employ his weapon. He must understand how to get in a good position from which to best engage the enemy and provide cover for his team. He must also understand the terrain he is in and see how it can be used to his advantage and to the advantage of the platoon—and how the enemy can also use terrain to their advantage if allowed to do so. The machine gunner must also understand his field of fire. Field of fire is the area of the battlefield a SEAL is responsible for, whether a street, hallway, valley, or cardinal direction. In that area, he must locate and engage the enemy. But field of fire is equally important in its limitations. Outside one's field of fire, there might be innocent civilians, other friendly forces, or perhaps even your own SEALs. Bluntly stated, staying within your field of fire prevents you from shooting your own people.

So the machine gunner can have a lot on his mind, but because his job is to shoot, there generally isn't much leadership required from him. Machine gunners are almost always part of a small fire team of four to six people, which is led by a fire team leader. With the lack of leadership opportunities, being a machine gunner is a job that is generally held by relatively inexperienced new guys who are in their first or maybe second platoons. Because of the size of the machine gun, it is often referred to as "the pig," which makes the machine gunner a "pig gunner." Also, because of the size of the pig gun, it usually requires a SEAL who is slightly larger to carry it. While it is not always true, it is common for new guys to be assigned as pig gunners if they are large-framed, strong individuals.

There is also an ongoing stereotypical joke in the SEAL Teams that pig gunners, being big, strong new guys, aren't the sharpest tools in the shed. Any new guy that does something dumb will be told he "will make a good pig gunner." When a briefing is completed, it would not be uncommon for the platoon chief to ask, "Do you pig gunners understand?"

This is why the stereotypical pig gunner makes the perfect example of Extreme Ownership—because the stereotypical pig gunner is going to make mistakes, and they are a very easy target for blame; I heard it on a fairly regular basis from young SEAL leaders on training operations that I ran. These young leaders didn't yet fully understand their roles and the concept of Extreme Ownership.

The training operations I ran were very complex and stressful combat simulations. We had a large budget for training, and we utilized it to replicate the chaos and mayhem of combat to the best of our ability. We hired Hollywood set designers to make our training areas look like cities or villages in Iraq or Afghanistan, we used role-players to mimic the actions of both enemy combatants and friendly civilians, and we simulated weapons with paintball or other high-end paint-marking rounds or with a multimillion-dollar laser tag system.

This simulated combat zone not only taught tactics, it was the ultimate leadership laboratory. And this is where I would see young SEAL leaders reveal that they didn't understand what Extreme Ownership really meant.

Let's say a young pig gunner shot his weapon in the wrong direction, outside his field of fire. When I would ask the pig gunner's leader what had gone wrong, it was very easy for him to say, "Well, the pig gunner made a mistake. He shot in the wrong direction."

"Whose fault is that?" I would ask.

"Well, the gunner aimed the weapon. He pulled the trigger. It is his fault."

"Actually," I would explain, "it is your fault."

"How can it be my fault? He's the one who shot the weapon!" the young leader would object.

This was a pretty common response. But it was also wrong.

You see, if a pig gunner makes a mistake, it means he hasn't been trained properly. The leader is responsible for training the gunner. If the gunner shoots in the wrong direction, it means he hasn't been briefed so he fully understands his field of fire. The leader is responsible for briefing the gunner. And yes, it could also mean the pig gunner is completely incompetent in understanding his task and knowing his field of fire. If that is the case, it is the leader's responsibility to identify that shortfall and either train the gunner so he does understand, remove the gunner from his position and place him into a job he is capable of, or, as a last resort, fire the gunner from the team if he cannot do his job properly.

So regardless of the reason the gunner failed, it is the leader's fault. A leader is responsible for everything a person on his or her team does. I even felt like this when one of my guys would get in trouble off base. If one of the SEALs who worked for me went out in town and drank too much and got in a fight, I always thought, *Where did I mess up? How did I fail to make that individual realize the consequences of his actions? Why didn't I know he was headed for trouble and keep him from going out?*

Taking Extreme Ownership means that leaders are responsible for every action the people on their team make. It is as simple as that.

There are some things that occur that are beyond the control of the leader, but they are far fewer than most people think. One great example of that is the weather. Everyone knows we can't control the weather, so if a mission has to be canceled because the weather is too bad for the helicopters to fly the assault team to the target, that obviously can't be the leader's fault. After all, the leader can't control the weather.

Wrong. While the leader can't control the weather, he can certainly put contingency plans in place in case there is bad weather. There could have been a backup plan using ground vehicles to get to the target. The leader could have forward staged closer to the target so helicopters weren't required. He could have even come up with a contingency timeline that kept all assets available if the weather turned bad so the mission could be delayed rather than canceled. So while the leader can't control the weather, he can certainly plan to deal with it.

This means there are no "buts" to taking Extreme Ownership. It applies to everything. And the moment a leader decides he is going to allow excuses, it opens up the door to shift blame onto others. That leads to failures.

PREEMPTIVE OWNERSHIP

When a leader knows they cannot blame anyone or anything else, they will implement what I call *preemptive ownership*—they will take ownership of things to prevent problems from unfolding in the first place. The leader who knows he can't blame his machine gunner when the machine gunner makes a mistake is going to take preemptive ownership and focus on training that machine gunner and ensuring he understands the plan and his part in it. The leader who knows bad weather is no excuse not to execute a mission will take preemptive ownership to ensure there are layers of contingency plans in the event the weather takes a bad turn.

The same is true for any team. If the leader knows there truly are no excuses, then he or she will make every conceivable effort to prepare. Ownership isn't just about taking responsibility when mistakes happen; the highest form of Extreme Ownership takes place preemptively, before the mistakes occur. So don't just take Extreme Ownership after the fact; take preemptive ownership to mitigate problems before they even happen.

TAKING OWNERSHIP WHEN BEING BLAMED

People often ask me, "How do I take ownership when other people are blaming me and saying things are my fault?"

To me, the answer is blatantly obvious. I tell them, "That's the whole point! When your team blames you, you say, 'Yes! Everything is my fault. I am the leader, and I am responsible for everything that happens—the good and the bad—and yes, this is my fault. And here is what I am going to do to fix it.'" Then I tell them to shift immediately to proactive problem solving and explain their solution or, if they don't have a solution, say they are trying to figure one out.

That answer—simply taking ownership—is obvious, but it can be a hard one to figure out. It is hard to do this, once again, because of our egos. It hurts our egos when we accept the blame and take ownership of it. Some people can't get over that hurdle. But it hurts even more when someone else is pointing their finger at us, assigning us blame for whatever the problem is. And when someone points their finger at us and blames us for a problem, what do we do? We get defensive. We all get defensive.

So the answer to this question is easy. When you are a leader and someone blames you for something going wrong, you accept the blame. You own it.

But what happens when you are the subordinate and your boss is blaming you for something that went wrong? Once again, the ego and defensive mechanisms will activate and make you want to deny or shift the blame onto other people. Overcome those impulses and take ownership. But what if it *really wasn't my fault*? What if the problem *really wasn't me*? I hear that objection all the time from people.

Let's take a look at that argument, once again using the machine gunner as the subject in question. Imagine you are in a four-man fire team. You are a basic rifleman. There is also a fire team leader, a machine gunner, and a grenadier. You patrol next to the machine gunner. During a training exercise, the machine gunner shoots outside his field of fire, endangering some friendly forces.

On the completion of the training exercise, your team leader says, "Why did you let the machine gunner shoot outside his field of fire?"

Now, from one perspective, this is ridiculous. You are a simple rifleman. You are not the leader. You are not the machine gunner. You are responsible for your own field of fire, not the machine gunner's; the machine gunner is responsible for his field of fire. On top of that, he is the one pulling the trigger. So how can you possibly be held responsible for the machine gunner's actions? So you let your boss know, "Hey, boss, the machine gunner is responsible for his field of fire, not me. You should go tighten him up." The fire team leader looks at you disappointedly and walks away. You feel strange that he looked disappointed, but you feel vindicated that you stood up for yourself and placed the blame where it should go—on the machine gunner.

This seems like it might have been the right move, but it wasn't. Here is another perspective. When the leader says, "Why did you let the machine gunner shoot outside his field of fire?" you realize that the fire team leader has higher expectations of you than being a "simple rifleman." The leader expects you to do more than just handle yourself; he expects you to help other members of the team, to help direct and lead the machine gunner. This is a compliment and a nod of confidence in your leadership skills. So you respond, "I'm sorry, boss. While I knew my own field of fire, I should have confirmed that the machine gunner knew his. It would only have taken me a second or two, and it would have ensured that he understood what was going on. It was my fault, and I won't let it happen again."

As soon as you finish that statement, the fire team leader nods with confidence. "Perfect. That's what I need. I need you to step up and lead. I can't be everywhere all the time. Thanks for helping out." The fire team leader pats you on the shoulder and walks away. You feel great. You realize your fire team leader has confidence in you and high expectations, and you also know that by being a leader, the whole team will do better. This was the right answer.

To throw one more perspective into this: What about the fire team leader? Who does he want on his team? The rifleman who evades the blame and shirks responsibility? Or the one who takes ownership of mistakes, even those made by someone else in the fire team? The answer is obvious: any leader wants people on his or her team that step up and take ownership. So be one of those people.

PICKING UP BRASS

Leaders might be above their subordinates in the rank structure, but they are not *actually superior* to those below them in the chain of command, and this means leaders must respect them. It also means there is no job too small or menial for a leader to do.

In the SEAL Teams, we shoot a lot of weapons on vast, highly dynamic ranges that cover dozens of square miles of land. When we shoot, the weapons leave behind brass shell casings by the hundreds of thousands, if not millions. Because brass has value and can be recycled, and because the training ranges must be kept clean, when a SEAL platoon finishes a block of training, it then has to pick up all those brass casings.

This is a pretty miserable task and usually takes a couple of days of gutting through high temperatures in the desert heat and crawling around on your knees picking up shell casings. It is a menial task that requires zero skill and no leadership whatsoever.

Because of that, it is very easy for a SEAL leader to leave the menial task of picking up brass to his subordinates. There is always administrative work that needs to be completed, meetings that need to be attended, and future operations that need to be planned. But leaving the brass for others to pick up is usually not the right call for a leader. I always picked up brass with my troops. Not only did it display that no job was above me, it was also a good time to interact with the frontline SEALs, bond with the subordinate leaders and troops, and observe how everyone interacts with one another. It also revealed who on the team was slacking.

Leaders who chose not to pick up brass missed out on all that. Sure, they may have attended yet another meeting in the vast pool of meetings, they might have finished their administrative work or gotten some additional sleep. But they didn't build relationships with their troops; they didn't see how their troops interacted; and they certainly didn't prove their humility to their team.

This is not to say the leader should always be in the trenches—that is not true at all. A leader has to lead. A leader does have to attend meetings, take care of administrative work, plan for the future, and attend to all kinds of pressing tasks. But there are times, especially when a job is particularly taxing on the troops, when it is important to get down in the dirt with the folks on the front line and *do work*.

This is similar to how a leader should treat high-risk operations or anything where there is a significant level of discomfort. If a team is being placed into harm's way on a regular basis, the leader must sometimes join the team in facing that risk. If there is a particularly hard job, a good leader should periodically go out and actually do that job. It is the same if there is a job that requires a high level of discomfort or suffering—the leaders should occasionally experience that suffering alongside the people who have to endure it every day. Whether it is repairing power lines in the freezing cold, pouring concrete in the extreme heat, patrolling a bad neighborhood as law enforcement, or even just bearing the constant rejection of cold calling for sales. In any of these cases, good leaders will do the hard things their subordinates do every day so they never forget to respect the job itself and the people who do the job, and also so the troops recognize the leader's willingness to shoulder some of the burden so he or she can understand the true challenges of the job.

LEADING FROM THE REAR

One of the most common mantras that leaders hear is "Lead from the front!" And it makes sense; after all, some critical things happen when leaders lead from the front.

When a leader leads from the front, he or she is setting the example, showing exactly what to do and how to do it. This model can be critical during fear-inducing moments There are many examples in combat where the situation is dire and it is leadership from the front that changes the outcome. Perhaps there is some open terrain to cross; maybe there is an enemy sniper waiting to take a shot; maybe there is a room with enemy fighters behind the door that needs to be entered. Any of these scenarios can cause people to become fearful and freeze. Who wants to risk death?

But any of these situations can grow infinitely worse if no action at all is taken. Those types of combat examples prove that someone needs to act. More often than not, that someone is the leader. When no one else has the courage to take action, the leader has to lead from the front. The leader has to charge across the open terrain, maneuver in the enemy sniper's line of fire, or breach the door to engage enemy fighters. If the leader doesn't take action, no one will. The troops will freeze, and the enemy will seize the initiative, get the upper hand, and win.

It is not only combat situations where leaders need to lead from the front. In any situation that has stagnated because of fear or apprehension, a leader stepping up and taking action is a solid solution. The same is true of terribly arduous tasks. People tend to shy away from suffering; they will procrastinate and avoid getting started. But when the leader jumps in and starts attacking the job, others will jump in and get started as well.

A leader must also lead from the front when it comes to setting a good example: treating people with respect, taking care of one another, and being professional at all times. If the leaders lead in this manner, others will follow.

Examples like these prove there are plenty of times when a leader must lead from the front. But there are also times when a leader must lead from the rear or perhaps from the middle.

From a tactical perspective on the battlefield, leading from the front increases risk to the leader. Sometimes it is necessary to take that risk, but if the leader is killed or otherwise incapacitated, that can be catastrophic to the team. A leader must be judicious about when and where to take risk. Beyond the risk, if the leader positions himself or herself at the front, he or she can easily become bogged down in the immediate tactical problem. When dealing with direct tactical problems like being in a firefight, the leader won't have much visibility beyond that, and that will cause decision-making to become difficult at best.

The same thing happens in the business world; if a leader gets into the weeds in minuscule details of day-to-day operations, then they lose the visibility of the broader events unfolding, and the decision-making process falls apart.

When I served as a SEAL assault force commander, I always tried to avoid being one of the first six to eight people to enter a potentially hostile building during an assault. I did this because the first six to eight people would be clearing rooms, perhaps getting in gunfights, and, at a minimum, detaining potentially resistant prisoners—in short, the first six to eight people would be heavily engaged in dynamic, fluid situations that required their full attention. If those first assaulters got into a firefight and were immersed in trying to stay alive and eliminate the enemy, who would call for supporting assets? If they were overwhelmed by a large number of detainees, who would call for reinforcements? If possible enemy personnel were seen departing the building, who would notify the external security elements that this was happening? In any of those cases, while the assault team was dealing with the immediate tactical problem, someone else had to lead. In those situations, it was on me to lead. My job was not to clear rooms, engage targets, or grapple with detainees. My job was to detach, assess all the dynamics of the situation, and get my men the support they needed.

So when I approached a building, if I happened to end up as one of the people toward the front of the assault team, I would step back, high port my weapon, and allow some of the other SEALs to go in front of me. As soon as my SEALs saw me do that, they immediately knew what was happening and would move past me toward the target. The momentum would not be broken.

It was the same thing if I happened to be holding security down a hallway or on a corner. My team knew I should not be holding security. Holding security requires 100 percent focus and the shooter holding security cannot look around to see what else is happening; he has to watch his designated area for threats. My men did not want me holding security, and they didn't want me staring down a hallway; they wanted me to organize supporting assets, to monitor reports about enemy activity, and to calculate our next move. They wanted me to lead. I couldn't do any of those things if I was holding security.

So when I did have to pick up security, one of my guys would almost instantly tap me on the shoulder, present his weapon to the enemy threat, and nod to indicate that he had the area covered now and had taken responsibility. Then I could back off, high port my weapon again, and pay attention to what was going on in the bigger picture.

If one of my guys saw me trying to get control of a detainee or marshaling a prisoner or clearing a room or a hallway, he would step in and do it for me. My team wanted me looking up and out, not down and in.

During immediate action drills for land warfare situations, I taught young SEAL leaders this same idea. They shouldn't always be at the front, engaging the enemy. Once the initial volley of fire is over and a call has been made, the leader should move out of the direct firefight to a good covered position so an assessment can be made and a call executed.

But it is not only on the battlefield where a leader has to be cautious about leading too far from the front. Planning is another time it is important to consider where to lead from. Instead of the leader coming up with the plan, the preferred method is to let the team members come up with it—let it be their idea. When the leader allows the team members to come up with the plan, those members have already bought into it; there is no need to convince them of anything. Of course, if the planning process gets bogged down or different members of the team can't agree on a course of action, it might be necessary for the leader to step in and provide guidance or even make a decision on which course of action to use.

But it is almost always preferred for the leader to lead from the rear, to allow the troops to take the lead on the plan and to take ownership of it. The best ideas often come from the people on the team who are closest to the problem; those are the folks on the front line. Don't inhibit them; instead, allow them the freedom and authority to create and execute new plans and ideas. They have the knowledge. Give them the power. Don't feel the need to always lead from the front. Take a step back and let your team lead.

DON'T OVERREACT

There are times when people will say and do things that make no sense. There are times when things will not go the way you want. When this happens, good leaders remain levelheaded. Don't get agitated. Keep your emotions in check. Take measured account of the situation. Keep your opinions to yourself as you analyze, logically, what is actually happening.

Remember that anything you might say at the moment is based on incomplete and likely inaccurate information. Allow for the situation to unfold and for a more solid picture to appear before you speak up.

This is not to say that there aren't some times when a quick decision needs to be made. But even in those cases, a pause must be taken to ensure you know what is really happening. Even in a gunfight, after the shooting starts you have to further assess what is happening. If you are being shot at from the north, you obviously need your team to begin returning fire to the north, but you can't immediately commit your forces to maneuvering on the enemy to the north. You have to estimate the size of the enemy force; if they appear to be small, perhaps you can attack and take them out. But if they are large, you might want to order your forces to break contact and leave the area. Once you have approximated the size of the enemy force, you have to assess the terrain and calculate if it makes sense to maneuver to the north. If there is nothing but open terrain with no cover and concealment, an attack on even a small enemy force might be futile, but if there is some terrain allowing movement toward the enemy, perhaps an attack is the right decision. Finally, you have to decide whether or not this is actually the main force of the enemy. Are these enemy to the north the main thrust of the enemy effort? Or are they just meant to distract you while a larger, more substantial force prepares to crush you from another area? Those are some things that must be considered. They must be considered quickly, but they must be considered fully and carefully to ensure a decision is the right decision.

In the business world, the same type of assessment needs to be done when anything goes wrong. If you hear an employee talking with a competitor and possibly leaving your ranks, there is no reason to fly off the handle. Instead, remain calm and dig for more information. If you are told that a project is significantly off track, don't start yelling and screaming. Instead, calmly determine what is causing the problem and what support is needed to get the project back on track.

There is no reason to overreact; overreaction is always bad. Not only does it lead to poor decisions, it also makes you look bad as a leader. People don't like it when leaders overreact; it means the leader is not in control and might make irrational, snap decisions. So take a step back, detach from your emotional reaction, find out what is really going on, and then make calm, logical decisions based on the reality of the situation.

DON'T CARE

There is another way to keep your reactions under control. It is another form of detachment, and it is a very hard form of detachment to master. It is a form of detachment called *I don't care.*

People are familiar with this idea in negotiations; it is the ability to walk away and it is a powerful weapon. "Oh, you don't want to lower your price? That's fine, *I don't care, keep it.*"

When you are a leader, not caring is a very powerful tool as well. You want to utilize your plan instead of mine? Cool, I don't care. You want me to do some crappy job for you that others find demeaning? Fine, I don't care. Oh, you want me to give someone else the opportunity to lead a project? Awesome, I don't care; I'll give them all the support I can.

Yes, the ability to not care goes a long way, but it is also a hard ability to acquire. Why? Because it requires being able to subdue and subordinate the most powerful driving force a human being has— their ego.

If you drill down on the things you care about, you will find that many of them are rooted in ego, even the simple examples I just gave above—being asked to do a crappy, demeaning task. Why does that make us mad? Because of our egos. A good leader in that situation can put their ego aside and simply get the job done, no matter how crappy the job is.

The next example is giving someone else the opportunity to lead a project. This will obviously make my job easier, as I will no longer have responsibility for the whole project. Then why do people object to letting someone else lead? Because it hurts our egos to give up leadership, and it hurts even more to give up leadership and then turn around and give support to the person who just took your leadership position. But it only hurts your ego.

When you dig deeper into what you care about, it is clear many of our feelings are tied to our egos, so we have to set them aside. Your ego drives you to want to win. It pushes you. It won't let you sleep. It doesn't care about anyone else. But if you really want to win, to achieve ultimate, strategic, long-term victory, you must override your ego. You have to learn to not care. Because ego can also be very shortsighted.

If you do the demeaning job, you show your humility and your willingness to sacrifice for the team. If you let someone else lead, you build trust and also reveal the confidence you have in your leadership capability. Those building blocks will propel you toward your ultimate goal and—here is the dichotomy—your ego will be satisfied. That's right; to actually win strategically in the long game, you have to not care. And to not care, you have to set aside your ego.

EVERYONE IS THE SAME, EVERYONE IS DIFFERENT

Everyone is the same, but everyone is different. The better a leader understands this dichotomy, the better he or she will understand people.

The first half of this dichotomy is that everyone is the same; there are archetypal people in every organization. You will see confident, natural leaders; shy loners who want to avoid the spotlight; quiet, cerebral thinkers; bold, aggressive individuals; people who want to win; and people who aren't very concerned about winning. It is easy to think about the most common categories of people; they exist in every group, from a SEAL platoon to a corporate boardroom to a Girl Scout troop. These characters are everywhere; people are the same.

But the other half of this dichotomy is that every person is different. They have different motivations, different agendas, different idiosyncrasies, and different ideas. As much as you can categorize someone as a "leader" or a "loner," they are all still completely different from other leaders and other loners you may have worked with.

These differences are among the things that makes leadership so challenging. As a leader, you have to connect with many different types of individuals. You have to learn to use different styles of communication with different people, but at the same time relay the same message. You have to interpret what drives an individual and incorporate that into your leadership strategy. You have to understand how much pressure an individual can take and how well they perform under that pressure. You have to do all this while maintaining a consistent message, an equitable distribution of your attention among your troops, and without getting so specific that everyone on the team becomes reliant on spoon-fed communications that are custom created for their individual needs.

This requires a leader to be like a fine woodworker, a craftsman who can shape wood into a useful object with a wide range of materials. He or she has to know not only what tools to use but also how those tools vary when being used on different types of wood, from a soft piece of pine to a hard slab of oak. Different types of wood require the application of different tools, just as different types of people require different tools of leadership. But it does not end there. Individual pieces of wood have their own unique characteristics; they have knots and splits and twists that must be handled correctly, lest they ruin the final product. Because of this, the woodworker cannot merely understand that different tools are required for different types of wood; he or she must know that various tools must be applied in distinctive ways to overcome the infinite number of one-of-a-kind pieces of wood that exist.

So while a piece of wood is a piece of wood, and all wood is the same fundamental type of material, there are different types of wood, and because of nature and circumstance and chance, each piece is completely unique. Every piece is the same, but every piece is different.

The same goes for human beings. Every person has some shared characteristics that make them human, but at same time, every person is a one-off, unique individual who requires handling specific to their singular nature.

What does this mean for the leader? Is a leader required to create custom applications of communication and interaction for every single individual he or she works with? Of course not. It is also where this attempt at leadership instruction falls short. It would be impossible to document the leadership-specific tools and then the particular application of those tools for every single type of individual in existence. But that is not the purpose of this instruction. The purpose is simply to provide awareness because it is very easy for a leader to mistakenly use all his or her leadership tools universally in all situations. The leader thinks that if a technique worked with one group, it will work with the next; if a tool worked on one person, it will work on the next person. And while success in the past certainly indicates a probability of success in the future, it does not *guarantee* it.

Too often, when leaders apply the same leadership tool in the same way that has worked for them in the past, they cannot figure out why their team or individuals on the team are not performing the way they had envisioned or the way a different team had performed when they had received the same leadership. In those situations, the leader may feel the team is at fault, so then the leader applies the same tools, but applies those tools *even harder*. But it doesn't help; in fact, the reaction from the team is pushed even further from the desired outcome. The leader, now even more upset and even more convinced that the team or the individuals are the problem, applies the same tool with maximum pressure. What happens then? Just as when a woodworker applies too much pressure with a tool and the wood splits or burns or warps and the wood is ruined, a team or some of the individuals on the team can be ruined if the leader's approach is inappropriate or is applied with the wrong amount of pressure.

The prudent leader does not do this. The prudent leader recognizes that the leadership tool being used is either the wrong tool or he or she is applying it in the wrong way. And then, instead of simply applying it in the same manner, but harder, a good leader will take the pressure off. He or she will assess the situation, look at the team and study the individuals that make up the team, and analyze the dynamics of the situation. Then the good leader will adjust the manner in which he or she is utilizing the tool or will try a completely different one.

What does this actually look like from a leadership perspective? Perhaps team members aren't taking any initiative, so the leader gives them more specific direction so they can begin to make progress. But instead of taking more initiative, they begin to take even less. So the leader gives them even more oversight to ensure they are moving forward. But this continues to make them even less proactive. So the leader applies maximum pressure, explaining exactly what he or she wants done, which leaves the team members with no initiative whatsoever. They are content to sit and wait to be told what to do.

A more prudent leader would have taken a step back and seen that his or her detailed instructions had become micromanagement, and instead of inspiring the team members' initiative, it was robbing them of it. Once the leader realizes that, he or she could move in the other direction, providing broad guidance and granting the team members the authority and autonomy to come up with their own way ahead, thereby giving them the ownership and inspiration to take initiative and make things happen.

The same thing can happen to individual members of a team: if an individual is not performing to their maximum potential, perhaps the leader decides to pull some responsibility away from that individual so they realize they need to improve their performance. But instead of improving, the individual loses confidence and begins to perform even worse. So the leader removes even more responsibility, which causes the same reaction, but on top of that, the worker begins to feel and show some resentment toward the boss. An antagonistic relationship forms, and the situation spirals downward.

But if the leader had paid attention and recognized the declining attitude of the individual in question, he could have shifted the approach. Instead of removing responsibility from the individual, the leader could have increased it, giving the worker some projects of higher importance that the individual would have to step up to execute. The worker then feels like the boss trusts him and believes he can do a good job, so the individual is motivated to put forth more effort and gains experience and confidence. When those projects are completed, the individual is likely to ask for more and have that request granted. The worker is now on the right path, moving forward and improving as an individual as he helps the team.

Of course, this is not always the case. Some individuals buckle under increased pressure; it takes them longer to gain confidence.

Other individuals see the loss of responsibility as a challenge—*I'll show you,* they think—so they work even harder to gain back their responsibility and prove they are worthy of even more. So different people in similar situations who have the same symptoms can require the opposite treatment. That is why different tools and careful application must be administered by the leader.

Just as a fine woodworker is not merely a craftsman but an artist, a leader cannot simply apply leadership tools universally and with indiscretion; a leader must apply them to teams and individuals with tact, diplomacy, prudence, and subtlety. That is the art of leadership.

LET NATURE WORK

People are the product of both nature and nurture. They are born with some attributes and develop and add to those attributes during their lives through training and experience. People have different personalities, motivations, temperaments, attitudes, skills, and aptitudes. Some of these traits come from their genetic pool; others, from their life experiences. It is unclear which traits come from nature and which come from nurture, or to what level nature and nurture impact the various traits.

Luckily, when you are a leader, your goal is not to understand where each person's traits came from but how best to utilize those traits to best benefit the team and, thereby, the individual. If possible, it is prudent to match the attributes with the job. Don't try to force a person into a role that is not suited to him or her. Don't make a shy introvert a salesperson. Don't put a brash, insensitive person in charge of human resources. Don't put a wildly creative person in a role that demands strict procedures, and don't put a highly meticulous perfectionist into some chaotic duty. Put people in roles that make sense for their personalities.

This is not to say people should be pigeonholed strictly into positions that perfectly suit their characters. This is an untenable goal; jobs will not always be ideal for everyone. Everyone will have to work outside their natural comfort zones from time to time, and they should also be placed outside their comfort zones to become better in their areas of weakness. It is the role of the leader to ensure this happens in a measured and controlled way.

So while a good leader might not permanently assign a shy introvert to a sales position, the leader should have them make some sales training calls so they become more comfortable talking to people. Over time, the shyness can be overcome, and the person is better equipped to expand their role. Likewise, a leader would not choose to put a brash and offensive person into a human resources role, but it would certainly be beneficial to do role-playing exercises with the brash person so they can learn to be more careful with their speech. The same goes for any personality type; to grow and learn, people must be assigned tasks that bring them outside their domain of competence.

While this is good for growth, people's primary duties should reflect what they are naturally suited to do. They will enjoy their work more and do a better job, and this will benefit them and the whole team. Don't fight against nature. Use it.

ISOLATION AS A LEADER

There is no doubt that as a leader, you have to be comfortable being alone; after all, you will likely have some level of separation from the troops. If you are not careful, it can be lonely at the top. You will have a tendency to be alone because you will likely be working more than anyone else, showing up earlier, and going home later than the rest of the troops.

You will also be alone with decisions, because as the leader, decisions are ultimately yours and yours alone. Sure, you can seek counsel and gain consensus, but when the final decision is made, it is made by the leader alone. That is the burden of command.

That being said, while leadership can be isolating, it does not have to be lonely. I was usually not lonely as a leader. As I developed my team and got to know them, I cultivated extremely strong relationships up and down the chain of command. Of course, this must be done with caution; a leader can't come out of the gates looking to befriend every individual on the team. Not every individual has the maturity and sensibility to have a close relationship with their boss. So you have to take it slowly as you build trust and relationships.

Eventually, you should end up with a few trusted agents at various levels of your organization. When you have established this, you can keep your fingers on the pulse of the team, become aware of possible problems that are forthcoming, and bounce ideas off others before you launch them. On top of all that, once you have established some close relationships inside the team, you have people to laugh and joke with and to vent to a little bit during stressful times. This will mitigate the feeling of loneliness at the top.

Of course, a leader must keep these relationships under control. Relationships *do not* mean preferential treatment. Relationships *do not* mean undue influence. And relationships *do not* mean unfiltered candor and completely revealing one's thoughts. It is a fine line. Since this line is not to be crossed, err on the side of professionalism. But try not to go it alone. Have some close relationships with some of the people on your team and get feedback and input from them.

At the same time, it is also important to remember that the decisions themselves fall on the leader alone. While it is great to bounce ideas off subordinates, develop plans and courses of actions as a team, and build consensus around what the final decision is, the final decision itself still rests with one person and one person only: the leader. This is not only due to the hierarchy of rank structure but also because there are some things that only the leader can fully understand, even if he or she tries to explain them in great detail. The position of leadership reveals a perspective that it is almost impossible for others to appreciate. For that reason, the leader must make the final decision. If the decision results in failure, it wasn't "the team's decision." No, it was the leader's decision. There is no escaping that reality; no matter how many advisors weighed in, no matter how much a leader was swayed by the arguments of their team, the ultimate decision rests solely on the leader and the leader alone. That is all there is to it.

KNOW WHAT IS IMPORTANT AND WHAT ISN'T

One of the things that distinguishes a black belt in jiu-jitsu from a white belt is the black belt's understanding of what is important and what isn't. A black belt sees past insignificant movements, ignores trivial actions, and focuses on what actually matters.

A good commander on the battlefield does the same thing. The commander can tell when enemy shooting is merely reconnaissance by fire. A good commander understands when enemy movement is just a ploy. A good commander ignores things that will not have an actual impact on the battle.

Like the black belt and the battlefield commander, any good leader must be able to do the same thing: discriminate between what is important and what is not.

For a leader in any situation, changes are everywhere, both external and internal. External changes can occur in the environment, the behavior of the enemy, the market, the weather, or in the timing of a scenario. Internal changes can be the emotions of individuals, relationship dynamics, or the morale of the team.

Change is the reality of life; almost everything is in a constant state of flux. And it is a crucial part of a leader's job to figure out which changes are important and which are mere distractions. This is not always easy to do. I see leaders get caught up all the time in things that do not matter. They waste their time and energy on meaningless events or minor problems that will not impact the overall results they are trying to achieve. A black belt in jiu-jitsu is a master of energy conservation; not one movement is wasted defending against attacks that do not matter. Leaders must learn to do the same thing.

To discriminate between things that matter and things that don't, a leader must detach, take a step back, and assess whether or not any detail in a situation matters. When a leader is directly involved in any problem and they immerse themselves in the minutiae of a situation, every problem seems important, every molehill looks like a mountain.

So a good leader detaches and elevates above the tactical situation, where they can see what really matters. Before they dive into a problem, they ask themselves questions. *How will this problem impact the team's strategic goals? Can it cause mission failure? Is it worth my time and effort to engage in it? How bad can it get if I leave it alone?*

The answers to such questions should make it obvious to a leader if a problem requires their involvement. A good rule to follow is that a leader should err on the side of not getting involved in problems; the goal is always to allow problems to get solved at the lowest level. When subordinates are solving low-level problems, it allows the leader to focus on more important, strategic issues.

Of course, there is a dichotomy to this. A leader can elevate themselves too far and fail to recognize the importance of problems. They might think solving a problem is below them or think it will go away if they ignore it. They might think a subordinate can handle a situation when it really requires the involvement of the leader. Any of these mistakes can result in a problem growing out of control, so there has to be balance. While a leader cannot be distracted by things that are unimportant, they must also know what is important and when it is time to step down into the tactical situation and get a problem solved before it gets out of hand. This is a challenging thing to do, and it can only be done if a leader properly detaches, assesses, and makes good, solid decisions about what is important and what is not.

PRINCIPLES

THE MOST IMPORTANT MEMBER OF THE TEAM

"You are the most important member of the platoon," I told the point man. "You are the one who leads us on patrol. You know where we are and where we are going. You guide us all through hazards and are the eyes and ears of the platoon when it comes to sensing danger like ambush or improvised explosive devices." It was the truth. We all counted on the point man.

I had a similar conversation with the radioman. "You are the most important member of the platoon. If we run into a large enemy force and we come under the threat of being overrun, it is the radio on your back and your ability to use it that is going to save us. Your ability to call for fire—to contact aircraft or tanks or other friendly forces to come and save us—is what will keep us alive in a desperate situation. It will all depend on you." This was also a true statement.

But it was also true for the medic, and I told him just that. "You know there is nothing more important than bringing our guys back alive. And if someone gets wounded, it will be you, and only you, who keeps him alive until we can get him to a surgical facility. You are the most important person in the platoon."

The list goes on. I told the machine gunners that they were the most important; without their putting down suppressive fire during a gunfight, our platoon would not be able to maneuver and survive. The rear security man was the most important because, much like the point man, he knew where we were going and what direction to take us if we got in a gunfight. And of course the enlisted and officer leadership heard the same thing from me—they were the most important individuals on the team because leadership is the most important thing on the battlefield.

So in the end, I would tell each and every member of my squad, platoon, or task unit that they were the most important person in the platoon—and I was never lying. Because at any moment on a patrol, any one of them could easily become the most important person. And if any one member of the platoon failed the team at a critical moment, it could be catastrophic.

This should be the attitude you take with any team: that every person's job is absolutely critical. Explain to them what happens if they don't do their jobs well. Explain to them, even the people with the most menial jobs, how their little jobs fit into the big picture and the strategic mission.

Everyone has the most important job. Let them know that.

SPAN OF CONTROL

How many people can you lead? While there are some loose rules around how many people should be in your span of control as a leader, the actual answer depends on some variables.

The first one that must be considered is what situation you are going into. If you are leading in a dynamic environment where you are directing demanding physical and mental tasks like combat, then the number needs to remain fairly small. That is why military units are based on four- to six-man fire teams. A leader in a combat scenario can only keep track of and direct four to six people, maximum. The noise, confusion, fog of war, distance, and the limitations of communications caused by all those factors prevent even the best leaders from trying to lead groups any larger than four to six people.

As a SEAL task unit commander with thirty-five to forty individuals (depending on augments attached to us for particular missions), I still only had to directly lead a few people at a time. The task unit consisted of two platoons, the platoon had two squads, and each squad had two fire teams. Decentralized Command meant that I never had to try to keep track of all forty people. In fact, I usually just had to keep track of two or three subordinate leaders.

The most obvious example of this was getting a head count—making sure we had all our people as we maneuvered on the battlefield. I didn't have to count everyone; I simply gave the signal for a head count, and each of the fire team leaders would make sure they had their four guys, which they could do quite easily, since they were almost always within visual and audible range of one another. A quick scan or barked roll call would have that answer in a matter of seconds. The fire team leaders would then pass that information up to their squad leaders. Next, the squad leaders, of which there were two per platoon, would tell their platoon commanders they had a full count in their squads. Within seconds of my inquiry, my two platoon commanders would be passing me the signal that we were "up," which meant we had all our people and could move. If we weren't up, I would also know that in a matter of seconds and could address it. Either way, getting a head count by utilizing subordinate leaders and Decentralized Command was infinitely better than those task units that tried to use another method, such as having each person count off or assigning a leader to walk around and count every single person.

It was also important that each fire team had a succession plan in place; if the leader was wounded, killed, or otherwise incapacitated, the next ranking leader in the fire team needed to step up and take over his responsibilities, which included getting the head count done. So leadership at every level is paramount for Decentralized Command to work. If a squad leader covered for incapacitated fire team leaders and tried to keep track of all eight to ten people in his squad, he wouldn't be able to do it that effectively; that is just too many people to control. He needed other members of the fire teams to step up. Once that happened, the problem was solved.

In a more administrative environment, some of the basic functions of leadership are easier—meaning it is easier for a leader to locate, communicate, and interact with his or her people—so a leader can control more people. But there are limits to that as well. Business leaders also face challenges. Their days are filled with meetings and calls, they also have to travel, and day-to-day functions of a business demand their time and attention. So while a business leader can lead more people than a battlefield leader, there is still a limit; generally, the limit is around eight to ten people. Beyond that, the leader simply doesn't have the time or bandwidth to keep track of the events occurring inside the worlds of their subordinate leaders.

The last factor in how many people a leader can control is the quality, experience, and level of trust he maintains with his subordinate leaders. The better the subordinate leaders, the less supervision and intervention they require from the boss. If I have a leader beneath me with whom I have worked for a while, who has a good understanding of the mission, and who does well interpreting my commander's intent, he or she will not need much guidance or oversight from me. If I have a whole team of good-quality leaders like that, I can supervise more of them, because they each necessitate much less attention from me.

Conversely, if my subordinate leaders are inexperienced, lacking judgment, and don't fully understand the mission and strategic objectives, then I will have to be much more engaged with them. I will need to monitor their actions much more closely, and the demands on my time will be higher. Obviously, if I am leading a group of subordinates like this, I will not be able to oversee very many, since they will require so much more from me.

The quality of your subordinate leaders will likely be somewhere in the middle. Some leaders will be experienced, highly trusted, and capable of working with very little guidance. You will have a few leaders at the other end of the spectrum who are not as practiced or proficient and will require constant oversight and supervision. And of course you will have subordinate leaders who rank somewhere in the middle, who are somewhat experienced and skilled but still not ready to fly on their own. Of course, your goal is to transition every leader on your team into one who needs very little guidance so they can make things happen on their own, which will allow you to look up and out instead of down and in. But that will take time, and it will only be possible if you have a limited number of subordinate leaders to invest your time and effort into.

If you end up with too many people under your control, it may be more effective for you to elevate a few of the high-potential troops to be leaders of some smaller teams beneath you. This allows you to quickly bring your span of control into a manageable number.

Regardless of how you organize, just be sure to keep your span of control limited so you actually have some control.

TAKING CARE OF YOUR PEOPLE WITH DISCIPLINE

Discipline is the best way to take care of your people.

From day one as a leader in the military, you are told over and over again that you have to "take care of your people." But some leaders get very confused about what that means. They think "taking care of your people" means making sure they are comfortable and happy, coddling them, giving them as much time off as possible, and not pushing them hard.

This is wrong. In fact, the opposite is true. In the SEAL Teams, if you really care about your people, you won't coddle them at all. You will push them hard. You will train them hard. You will make sure they understand the tactics of war and the weapons and radios they will operate. You will ensure they are in top physical condition and prepared for the mental and emotional stress of combat. You will do everything in your power to prepare them for combat so you can give them the highest probability that they and the rest of the team return from the battlefield. If you really care about your people, you want them to go home to their families. The best way to make that happen is through the hard training that comes from discipline.

The same thing is true in business. While lives may not be on the line, if you really want to take care of your people, you need to push them. You need to make sure they understand their jobs. You need to drive them toward their goals. If they fail professionally, they fail to achieve their financial goals and cannot take care of their families or provide for them the way they want to. So when you are a leader, the best thing you can do is push them toward their goals.

Of course, this drive must be balanced. You cannot drive your people so hard that you break them. Burnout is a real thing, and it happens on the battlefield and in business. Be cautious about that, and don't let it happen. Taking care of your people also means knowing when to back off and when to give them a break. (See the section on handling stress on page 240.)

But don't think your job is to allow your people to take the easy path. The easy path leads to misery. The path of discipline leads them to freedom.

IMPOSED DISCIPLINE

Optimal discipline in a team is not imposed by the leader; it is chosen by the team itself. Optimal discipline is self-discipline.

But teams do not always have self-discipline; they may not understand the rewards that come with it. When that happens, it may be necessary for a certain level of discipline to be carefully applied and imposed so the team understands the benefits.

Perhaps there is a new, more rigid process a leader is trying to get his or her team members to adopt. But, as is common with change, they are resistant. Let's say the leader does the right thing and explains the *why* behind the change and clearly states the advantages that will come with its implementation. But, despite this information, the team members' attitudes do not change; they refuse to impose discipline on themselves.

At this time, with caution, the leader must apply pressure. "Listen, we have to give this a try to at least get some feedback," or "We need to give this a try before the company wastes more money on it," or "If we don't make changes, we are going to fall behind, and it is going to cost us all." Any of these statements are relatively soft ways of pushing the team to try the new process.

Why not just order them to implement the new method? Why not just force discipline upon them? If you know you are right, why not? Unfortunately, that is the least effective way to implement change. When you give that direct order and impose your will on the team, you are removing your subordinates' input from the equation. They are simply doing what you told them to do with zero control or contribution. When people have no input, they have no ownership; when they have no ownership, they have no personal stake in driving mission success. As soon as they hit resistance, they will stop forward progress.

Instead, it is infinitely better to get people to change voluntarily, to embrace the change and take ownership of it so they can drive toward success.

Look at the simple example of physical exercise. Sure, you can make people show up and do it, but you will not get maximum effort from them. Maximum effort can only come from the individual, and they will only put forth maximum effort if they actually want to. Otherwise, they will always be holding back and staying in their comfort zones. Progress will be limited.

But someone who wants to exercise will put forth real effort because the desire comes from them. The best-performing athletes in the world reach greatness because of how hard they push themselves, not how hard others push them. This is not to say athletes don't need coaches. Coaches absolutely play a huge role in the success of athletes. And obviously, sometimes coaches need to push players to do an extra workout, to run a play another time, to do the extra rep. Yes, that is imposed discipline, and sometimes coaches must impose it on their athletes.

But if the player has no say whatsoever, they will not respond properly. They have lost control over their own fate, and morale will begin to slide. So sometimes when a player wants to take a break or run certain drills or have a day of active rest, the coach should allow it.

A leader should do the same thing. The more control a leader can put into the hands of his or her subordinates, the better.

Of course, this doesn't always work, and there are times when the team members simply cannot identify the benefits they will receive by carrying out a task or implementing a change. When they fail to make that connection, they will not execute on their own, despite all the soft encouragement of the leader. This should be a rare case, because after all, if what the leader is pushing for makes sense, it should not be that hard to explain the sensibility of the decision to the team.

But if the leader cannot get the team to budge, sometimes the leader simply has to say, "We are going to do this." Again, this should be an extremely rare case; I can count on one hand the number of times I was forced to impose my plan on the team while I was in a leadership position in the SEAL Teams. Think about it: if what I am trying to do is going to benefit our team in accomplishing our mission, why wouldn't the team be on board? That is what makes this occasion so rare. But there are cases when individuals on the team have agendas that are not aligned with the leader's or the mission's. Those are the cases that might require a direct order.

Once a direct order is given, use caution. If team members are directed to do something against their will, they may well not want it to succeed. They will likely not put forth their maximal effort to achieve mission success, or, even worse, they may sabotage the mission just to prove their leader wrong. This is a worst-case scenario and is one of the reasons why imposing discipline on the team is never the best option. Of course, sometimes it has to be done, and in the best scenarios, the leader hopes the team accepts the discipline, sees the benefits of it, and eventually applies it voluntarily themselves.

Always remember that imposed discipline is an uphill battle; it is not the best way to lead. Instead, whenever possible, explain the *why*, make sure the team members understand the benefits to the mission and to themselves and, finally, give them as much ownership as possible so they execute driven not by imposed discipline but by the will of their own intrinsic discipline.

PRIDE

Pride is one of the seven deadly sins, and yet it can be a powerful force for good. The dichotomy between these opposite ends of the spectrum can be hard to understand and rein in properly. Pride can tear apart individuals and teams, yet it can also be an aspirational influence that drives successful positive behavior.

The term *pride* can be interpreted different ways, and even the same exact statement about pride can have different meanings depending on how it is construed. For instance, the phrase *He took a lot of pride in how he looked* could mean that an individual presented himself professionally and confidently and took solid care of his health, fitness, and hygiene. But it could also mean that he spent too much time focused on how he looked, implying that he was constantly in front of the mirror, enthralled by his own appearance.

The same can be said about a team. On one hand, excessive pride can lead to arrogance. Group members can become so convinced of their own greatness that they no longer feel the need to work hard, practice, rehearse, and try to improve. Their pride means they don't respect the people they are competing against. When pride becomes arrogance, the ego inflates, stagnation ensues, and the downward spiral begins.

On the other hand, pride can also be an immensely positive asset for a team to have. Pride can be the guiding, unseen force that keeps team members working hard, giving their best effort, and holding themselves and others on the team to the absolute highest standard. "Have some pride in your work" is a common admonition to an individual or team whose performance is lackluster; it means you need to actually care about what you are doing and then do your best.

When team members have pride, they put in the extra work, care about the details, and, accordingly, tend to perform at a much higher level than a team or organization without pride. This is plain to see within military units that have a high level of pride. Their exceptional standards are visible in everything they do—the way their soldiers look, the way they execute their missions, and even the way they carry themselves. *Unit pride* is a term that is used in the military and, while not perfectly quantifiable, is certainly observed and measured by everyone who has ever worn a uniform. Things like unit patches, songs, and banners are specifically designed to increase unit pride by creating a sense of belonging and an attitude of exceptionalism.

Unit pride comes from history. It comes from past performance. The more team members go through together, the closer they will bond and the more pride they will have. The tougher the challenges unit members face, the stronger unit integrity they will build, as long as the challenge doesn't break them.

Much of the pride in a military unit is derived first from what the unit has been through—the wars it has been in, the historic battles it has fought, the decorations and accolades it has received. When I was deployed to Iraq, it was common for U.S. Army and Marine Corps units to bring historical documents on deployment with them to hang on the walls of their tactical operations center, their chow halls, or their ready rooms. Unit flags and battle streamers would be ceremoniously positioned in prominent locations in barracks or briefing rooms. It was impressive to see.

Sports and business teams do the same thing. Banners of past victories are hung in stadiums and adorn hallways. Trophies are put on display in glass cases. In businesses, positive articles are framed and hung up. Awards are displayed on bookshelves and desktops, and good reviews are posted on walls.

When the past is held up and put on display in honor, it becomes the standard for all to pursue. Ideally, the goal is to have the team members strive for that high standard individually—to have them hold themselves and one another to that level of excellence. Optimally, a leader doesn't have to constantly police infractions and motivate them to give their best; if there is pride, the team polices itself. The team will not allow substandard performance. Anyone who slacks off is corrected not by the leadership but by the team itself. That is the power of pride.

What, then, of a team that lacks pride? Perhaps it doesn't have a storied history; perhaps it doesn't have a history of victory to hold high. What then?

It is one of the most critical tasks as a leader to instill pride in your team. How do you do that? How can you build the morale of troops and create the strong bonds of pride that result in an attitude where everyone on the team gives more than what is required?

The answer is simple; you give them the opportunity to earn it. Pride does not develop simply by telling team members that they are great or by hanging up banners. All the banners and signs and flags mean nothing if they aren't earned. To build pride within a team, you have to put the members in situations that require unity, strength, and perseverance to get through. You have to push them in training to the point where they are truly tested, and in that they will develop pride in what they have accomplished.

If you look at the military, it uses hard training to instill pride in various units. From basic infantry training, to airborne school, to the special operations selection courses, the hard training not only prepares the soldiers for combat, it also instills pride.

When I was a task unit commander, we trained harder than the other task units at our SEAL Team. We showed up earlier. We went home later. We did extra iterations of shooting and maneuvering. We trained in jiu-jitsu in the early mornings and then pushed hard during team physical training. We were disciplined. At first, I imposed the discipline, and there were some grumblings: "Why do we need to do this extra work?" and "What is the point in training so hard?" and "We shouldn't have to do this."

But over time the complaints faded, my imposed discipline turned into the team's self-discipline, and that self-discipline ultimately turned into pride. "We work harder than anyone else at this team," and "No one else comes close to our task unit," and some of the guys even said things like, "If you aren't in Task Unit Bruiser, you wish you were," which was said as a joke but with more than a hint of truth.

That was pride. And, of course, the harder we trained, the better we performed—not because we had more talented SEALs than the other task units but because we worked together more, prepared more, and held one another to a higher standard. The discipline I had imposed on them became internalized; it became self-discipline.

Everyone in the task unit did their job and then some. People weren't late. No one forgot gear. People paid attention during briefs. When there was something that needed to be done, someone did it. My guys did all the little things that make a good SEAL task unit, and they did them because of discipline and pride in Task Unit Bruiser.

If you want to build pride, you have to bring pain. Pride comes from shared suffering. Sure, pride comes from history, and pride comes from winning, but you can't count on that. If you want your team members to have pride, you have to make them earn it through hard work.

Of course, you can take this too far. You can work your team members so hard that they break. Instead of forging a team hardened by training and adversity, you can beat your team members so hard that you break their spirits instead of building their pride.

You can also build their pride up so much that they become arrogant. Sure, you want team members to think they can do anything, but take that too far and they think they are invincible. They might think they don't have to earn that pride through hard work, and they might slack off.

Don't let these things happen. Don't push the team members so hard and give them such harsh challenges that you break them, but don't give them such easy challenges that they completely dominate to the point that they think they don't need to train and prepare anymore. When you are pushing a team hard to develop pride, you have to use caution. If you see the morale of the team fading or you see frustration start to become the prominent attitude, you need to back off. Let the team get some wins. Contrarily, if the team members are winning so much during training that they start to think they don't need to prepare or they think they can't be beaten, they need to be put in check. They need to get pushed harder, so push them harder. No pride is built on easy wins, but a team has to win some to have some pride. Try to find that point, and fight to maintain it.

Pride is an awesome force as long as it is balanced between humility and confidence. If you let it creep too far in either direction, it will become destructive. It is on you to build, maintain, and channel that force: *pride*.

GIVING ORDERS

When I came home from my first deployment to Iraq where I served as platoon commander and took over as the commander of Task Unit Bruiser, my experience as a leader in training and combat was more extensive than the rest of the guys in the task unit. As a prior-enlisted SEAL leader who had taught the tactics for all the various mission sets that SEALs are responsible for, I had a very solid understanding of how to plan and execute an operation. As part of one of the earliest platoons to deploy to Iraq, I tested and affirmed my knowledge in combat operation after combat operation as we took down target after target all over Iraq. So when it came to planning missions, I had things dialed in. I knew how and where to deploy troops, the best timelines to follow, and how to most efficiently conduct actions at the objective.

But, as task unit commander, when it was time to give mission orders, I did not dictate to my subordinate leaders what troops to bring and where to put them. I didn't tell them how many vehicles to use or what weapons to carry. I didn't order timelines to follow or routes to and from the target to use or what contingencies to prepare for.

I didn't tell my platoons any of those details. If I did, the plan for the mission would not be theirs but mine. Instead, when giving orders, I would simply tell them what the mission objective was—the goal I wanted the platoons to accomplish. This is what the military refers to as Commander's Intent.

When I did this, it allowed the platoon leadership and the other SEALs in the platoon to come up with a plan themselves. They chose what troops to bring and where to put them. They chose how many vehicles and which weapons to bring. They figured out the timeline and the routes and the contingencies they needed to prepare for. And when they did all that, the plan became *their* plan, not mine—which means they *owned* it.

Now, this doesn't mean you will always agree with your subordinates' plan; I know I would often look at my subordinates' plans and know I had a better way. Sure, that might have been some ego, but it was also based on the fact that I had much more experience than anyone who worked for me. I had simply been in the SEAL Teams longer and had more opportunity and experience planning and conducting operations. But even if I had a plan that I felt was slightly better than my subordinates', I wouldn't override them. I would go with it; I would allow them to execute it. If I had a solution I estimated to be a 90 percent solution and saw that their plan was only an 80 percent solution, I would still let them execute their plan instead of mine. The commitment they would have when they executed their own plan would easily make up for the 10 percent loss in efficiency.

If my subordinates' plan was only a 70 percent solution versus my

90 percent solution, I would still let them execute it, but only after I gave them some small course corrections to make it more efficient. If their plan was even worse—let's say a 50 percent or 60 percent solution—then I would give them slightly bigger course corrections to get them on track and bring it to a 70 or 80 percent solution. Even then, it was still their plan, and they would execute it with conviction.

Now, if their plan was simply terrible with almost no redeeming qualities, then I would ask them questions until they realized how bad it was—and if a plan was not a good solution to the problem, it wasn't ever very hard for them to see their plan's shortfalls. Even then, instead of me then forcing my plan on them, I would have them go back to the drawing board, take the lessons they had just learned from their bad plan, and come up with a new one of their own. Once again, this allowed them to have true buy-in and ownership of it.

So when the opportunity is available, let your subordinates come up with the plan. Not only will it result in their taking ownership and buying into it, it will also give you the standoff distance and altitude you need to see holes in it. By not getting into the weeds, you can stand back and be the tactical genius.

All of this is easier said than done, and the biggest obstacle in allowing subordinate leaders to come up with a plan is your ego. Leaders want to be in control. Leaders want the troops to listen to what they say. Leaders often see themselves as the only ones actually capable of coming up with the right plan. All those thoughts and feelings are driven by the ego. Let it go. When your subordinates come up with a plan, even if it isn't as good as the one you have in your head, let your own plan go. *Let it go.* Be overjoyed that your subordinates have a plan that is at least somewhat workable. Make whatever minor adjustments are required, and then let them run with it. They will push hard to make it a success.

And with each iteration of planning they conduct, and with each correction you give them, they will become better. And soon, their plans will be as good as yours, if not better. When that happens, you can begin to look up and out instead of down and in, which is exactly what a leader should be doing.

YES-MEN

As a leader, you should not want to be surrounded by yes-men— people who agree with everything you say. As a subordinate, you should not be a yes-man; you should speak up when something doesn't make sense.

This concept sometimes worries leaders, because essentially what I am saying here is that subordinates should always be pushing back against their leaders, always asking their leaders why things are being done a certain way, and always offering up information and recommendations from their perspective on the front line. That scares some leaders. Some leaders would rather just have their subordinates do exactly what they are told to do.

That is a bad idea. As an example, let's say I am commanding three platoons out on the battlefield, and I am toward the rear of the formation. The lead element, first platoon, suddenly gets fired on by an elevated enemy position with several solid bunkers and multiple machine guns with interlocking fields of fire. First platoon retreats to a small depression safe from the machine-gun fire. They report back to me that they have received fire from the enemy, but I am anxious and want to move forward, so I reply to the first platoon commander with an order: "Take your platoon and assault and destroy the enemy bunkers." The order is simple enough: attack. But there is a major problem.

Attacking multiple enemy bunkers up a hill, in the open, when the enemy has several machine guns with interlocking fields of fire is not just a bad idea, it is a horrible one. Every person who assaults that bunker will die. The last thing in the world I want is a subordinate who simply says, "Roger that, sir," and leads everyone in his platoon to their deaths. No, I want a subordinate who has the confidence and the trust in me to say, "Boss, that isn't a good idea. We need to get some heavy artillery on the bunkers; then we can move around to the flank to take them out." If I am a good boss, I will listen to my subordinate, who is actually closer to the problem and therefore has a better understanding of it, and do what I can to support his suggestion.

This tactical example carries through to all kinds of different situations in planning, preparation, and execution. If you want optimal performance, don't just count on your own brainpower. Instead, encourage the rest of your team to think and to question you. Don't surround yourself with yes-men. They do nothing to help you or the team. And if it makes you uncomfortable to get pushback or questions from your team, check your ego; it is probably a little inflated.

THE EXCEPTION TO NO BAD TEAMS, ONLY BAD LEADERS

In *Extreme Ownership*, we wrote that there were "no bad teams, only bad leaders." We were not the first people to make this claim. Napoleon said there were no bad regiments, only bad colonels, and U.S. Army colonel David Hackworth said in his book *About Face* that there were no bad units, only bad officers.

Yet there are still people who feel that a "bad team" is a legitimate excuse for bad performance. That is simply not true. There are no situations and no exceptions where a subordinate is ultimately responsible for the performance of a team. It is always the leader's fault.

That being said, there is an exception to the rule that there are no bad teams, only bad leaders. The exception is that it is possible to have a *good team* that delivers outstanding performance despite a *bad leader*.

How does that happen if leadership is the most important thing in the success or failure of a team? It happens when there are subordinates in the team who lead regardless of their rank; they are tactful individuals who know how to lead despite not having been given the official authority. These subordinate leaders have found ways to lead without offending the structural leader, because the structural leader might not be able to deal with someone below them in the chain of command running things. If the structural leader has a big ego, they likely won't listen to any of their subordinates. For that reason, in a successful team that is being led by the junior people, the structural leader does deserve credit for having the humility to let his or her subordinates run things. Without humility, the structural leader would resist subordinates who try to lead; this would ultimately counter the efforts of those subordinates, and the team would fail.

Because of this exception to the rule, it means that just because a team is performing well, it does not necessarily mean the leader is the driver of that success. Sure, the leader might have the sense to step back and let other members of the team lead—which is a positive quality—but they aren't the ones actually driving the success; they are not responsible for it.

This is important because the next leader up the chain of command above that successful team must understand what is making the teams within his or her team successful; he or she must know the true strength of a team. Why? Because teams and organizations are not stagnant. Things change. Tasks shift. Missions are altered. And in all those cases, there are times when personnel must be moved, teams must be broken down and re-formed with different people, or promotions must be made. If a leader does not understand what is driving the success of a subordinate team, managing these changes can be problematic. A leader might want to strengthen a weak team and therefore move the leader from a strong team to the weak team. But if the leader of the strong team wasn't the driving force of success in the strong team, this move will make little difference for the weak team. However, if a leader can identify that it is actually a subordinate in the strong team who is driving the success, then promoting that subordinate into a leadership position in the weak team can turn things around. And there is a likelihood that because the strong team has sustained performance and intimate knowledge of how to be successful, they will continue to perform well despite losing their star player.

So while it is important to recognize that leadership is the most important factor in the success of any team or organization, it is also important to remember that leadership may not always come from the structural leader sitting on top of the wire diagram. While a bad team is without question the result of a bad leader, a good team is not necessarily the result of a good leader. You must know your people well enough to recognize and capitalize on that fact.

PART 2

LEADERSHIP TACTICS

BECOMING A LEADER

HOW TO SUCCEED AS A NEW LEADER

Once you have been selected as a leader, it is time to lead. What is the best way to do this? Like many things, starting off on the right foot is simple, but not easy. Here are some fundamental rules to keep in mind as you take command:

1. Be humble. It is an honor to be in a leadership position. Your team is counting on you to make the right decisions.

2. Don't act like you know everything. You don't. The team knows that. Ask smart questions.

3. Listen. Ask for advice and heed it.

4. Treat people with respect. Regardless of rank, everyone is a human being and plays an important role in the team. Treat them that way. Take care of your people and they will take care of you.

5. Take ownership of failures and mistakes.

6. Pass credit for success up and down the chain.

7. Work hard. As the leader, you should be working harder than anyone else on the team. No job is beneath you.

8. Have integrity. Do what you say; say what you do. Don't lie up or down the chain of command.

9. Be balanced. Extreme actions and opinions are usually not good.

10. Be decisive. When it is time to make a decision, make one.

11. Build relationships. That is your main goal as a leader. A team is a group of people who have relationships and trust one another. Otherwise, it is just a disconnected, incoherent cluster of people.

12. Lastly, get the job done. That is the purpose of a leader—to lead a team in accomplishing a mission. If you don't accomplish the mission, you fail as a leader. Performance counts.

These are straightforward rules. They make sense on paper, but they can be hard to remember and implement in a leadership environment. Review them often. Look at them in the morning, before meetings, and when you are about to make things happen. Review them before you go to sleep at night. Soon they will become second nature, but if you find yourself struggling, pause, read these rules again, and ensure that you are following them.

Sometimes, you have to step into positions where you might not have the knowledge or experience. That's okay. No one expects you to know everything. *You just got there.* You need time to learn.

That being said, while you might not know everything, you should be as prepared as possible. You should know the terminology. You should understand the fundamental principles of what your team is responsible for. You should know the names and faces of the people on your team. Study any documentation you can that will familiarize you with the mission. Being new is not an excuse for ignorance or lack of preparation.

If you have studied and you are prepared, then the questions you ask will be smart and well received. Ask to be shown how things work. Learn to operate the equipment; you will not be as proficient as the actual operators, but go through the motions so you understand them at a deeper level. Interact with the troops on the front line. Find out their challenges. Ask details about what they do and how they do it. Your interest in their job will increase their respect for you and will help build a relationship with the troops, which is the goal of a leader.

HOW TO BE CHOSEN TO LEAD

The number one way to give yourself a chance for a promotion and leadership is simple and straightforward: performance. Do your job well. Work hard. Be the first person to show up to work and the last person to leave. Volunteer for the most challenging tasks, projects, and missions that no one else wants to do, including those that are simply mundane and unrewarding.

The next thing to do to be selected as a leader is to not focus on yourself; don't make being chosen as a leader your goal. Instead, make your goal *helping the team win*. Don't feel you need to be the person in charge of everything. When someone else has stepped up and taken the lead, then be a good follower. The more you help the team win, the more people will want you on the team. The more people see you being humble and not clamoring for the spotlight, the more trust and clout you gain.

Of course, you can be too humble. If you constantly defer from accepting leadership opportunities and always let someone else take the lead, you might give the impression that you don't want to lead, which will result in you not being put into leadership positions. So, as I said, volunteer to lead whenever possible, but don't make that your primary focus. Make your primary focus helping the team accomplish its goals. This attitude will eventually get noticed, and you will get your chance.

WHEN YOU ARE NOT CHOSEN

There are times when you will not be selected as a leader. Perhaps they promote someone else from your team; perhaps they bring in someone from outside your team or outside the organization to lead. When that happens, you might feel frustrated or angry because you were not chosen. Keep those feelings to yourself.

Instead of allowing yourself to become angry and frustrated, take the opportunity to do a good, honest assessment of yourself to see why you were not chosen. After you have done that (and after you have given yourself time to calm down), you can even ask your superiors why you were not selected for promotion. Of course, this must be done with tact.

- *Don't say, "Hey, boss, why wasn't I selected for promotion? I am just as good, if not better, than the person you gave the role to."*
- *Instead, say, "Hey, boss, I wanted to get some feedback from you. As you know, there was a recent promotion here, and I eventually want to move up into a more senior leadership position too. I want to know if there is anything I can focus on or do better so I am more qualified and more prepared to lead when the next opportunity comes."*

And when you receive that feedback, *actually listen to it.* After all, you just asked for it! As human beings, we have a strong tendency to get defensive. Don't. Instead of getting defensive, listen, *truly listen,* and try to understand the perspective being offered. Then take ownership of those shortfalls and try to make improvements in the areas of critique you have received.

You must also understand that not all leaders are good at giving feedback; giving direct feedback is hard for some people to do. When you ask for honest feedback, you might not get it. You might be told, "Oh, you're doing great. It just wasn't your time." *This is not necessarily true.* You have to remember that there must be some reason you were not promoted, so do an even harder self-assessment and really dig down and analyze where you can improve.

Finally, *do not* hold a grudge against the person who got the promotion. As much as it pains your immature ego, support them. Make them look good. Help them win. Undermining them is going to hurt the team, make you look bad, and create an antagonistic relationship with that individual. Instead of moving closer to a leadership position, you will be moving away from it. Be a team player, and help the team and the new leader win.

IMPOSTER SYNDROME

Some people worry they aren't ready for a leadership position. Some even feel once in that position that they don't deserve to be there. These anxieties are often described as *imposter syndrome.* But while some people worry about this feeling, I actually believe it can be a good thing.

If you are worried that you aren't ready for a leadership position, that means you are humble. If you are nervous, it means you are going to do your best to prepare for the leadership role, and once in it, you are going to be thoughtful about your words, actions, and decisions. All these things are positive.

When I was an assistant platoon commander, a platoon commander, and a task unit commander in the SEAL Teams, I always felt the same way. I felt like I wasn't quite ready or wasn't quite capable of doing the job that was being asked of me. The burdens of command and the responsibility for my men and the mission were heavy and made me nervous about my decisions and actions. Because of that feeling, I doubled down on preparation. I focused on learning as much as I possibly could about strategy, tactics, and leadership. I wanted to do a good job.

This is the opposite of some SEAL leaders I worked with or put through training who thought they were not only ready but eminently qualified to do the job. In their minds, they didn't need to prepare. They didn't need to study. They didn't need to carefully consider their words and actions. And they didn't feel they needed to listen to anyone up or down the chain of command. That kind of attitude is the opposite of the imposter syndrome; it is just plain arrogance, and it will destroy a leader and a team. Going to the extreme and becoming overconfident is a disaster.

Of course, going too far in the other direction is a problem as well. The lack of confidence a leader shows if they don't believe they should be in a leadership position is obvious to every member of the team. So a leader has to balance between being too confident and not being confident enough.

If you feel you are getting too confident, simply take a step back.

Listen to others. Don't judge. Let subordinates step up and lead. This problem is relatively simple to solve as long as you have the sense to recognize that you are becoming too cocky and arrogant.

To sense this, you have to be aware of indicators that this is happening. One of the first warning signs is an attitude from the team members. Your big ego will brush up against theirs and cause friction. That is not good. You should not have friction from your troops. This is not to say you won't get pushback and suggestions and even disagreements; but all of those should lead to productive conversations where both sides learn and eventually agree. If you can't get them to agree with your ideas, that is a problem. And the problem is likely you. If your team members want to do something a certain way, your goal should be to *let them do it that way.* As long as their plan or idea has a decent chance of success, try to let them execute it. Of course, you can give guidance that will increase their likelihood of success, but keeping the core plan will give them ownership and appease their egos. This obviously only works if you put your ego in check. If you can't do that and you force your plan down their throats, they might execute it, but they will do it begrudgingly compared to how they would execute if it were their plan.

Another warning sign to recognize is a complete lack of resistance from the team members. This can occur if you are overconfident and look down on others. Your team members will not propose new ideas or offer suggestions because they know they will be shot down. This phase might come after you have denied their plans and ideas a few times and given no ground. They recognize that they cannot contend with your giant ego, so they shut down. It is up to the leader to recognize when they have gone too far, become over-confident, and allowed their ego to get the best of them.

But the opposite is true with the imposter syndrome when the leader's ego isn't strong enough and confidence is low. The team doesn't respect the leader's ideas and shuts him down at every corner. The solution is counterintuitive. People with imposter syndrome tend to clam up and recede—become invisible—which only invites more disrespect from the team. A leader with imposter syndrome should open up. Ask questions. Find out why a certain team member did a certain thing at certain time. Ask for input about a plan. Solicit advice on how to best move forward.

This is an important lesson for leaders, especially new leaders stepping into a new role. You don't know everything. No one expects you to know everything. But if you try to act like you know every-thing, the troops will see you for what you are: an imposter.

If you act humbly and expose yourself, ask questions, and admit that you don't know everything, you will start to build trust and confidence from the team.

This is not to say you get a free pass to be stupid and ask dumb questions. For leaders, there is such a thing as a dumb question. If you haven't taken the time to research as much as you can, if you haven't looked through manuals, read operating instructions, stud-ied the names and basic qualifications of the team—basically, if you haven't done your homework, the team will see just that: you didn't care enough to invest in understanding the mission, the gear and equipment, and, most important, the people. That lack of preparation shows the team you don't really care.

So stay humble, study, ask questions, learn, and balance the dichotomy between too much humility and too much confidence.

In a similar vein, there are people who hesitate to volunteer or accept a new leadership position, but there is nothing abnormal about feeling you aren't quite ready for one. Like I said, that is normal; if you are a humble person, which you should be, you will rarely, if ever, feel completely ready to move into a leadership position, so you must have faith in yourself and in the leaders above you who are offering one to you. You have to trust that they see you are ready and that is why they are asking you to step up.

INSECURITY AS A LEADER

If the imposter syndrome gets in a leader's head, it can grow very quickly into true insecurity, which is problematic. If it isn't controlled, it can begin a downward spiral for the leader and then the team.

But the problem comes not from feeling insecure in your leadership ability, experience, and knowledge; that is just humility. The problem comes when you inevitably try to cover it up. You shift conversations, avoid questions, and utilize other means of subterfuge to mask your weaknesses. But you won't be fooling anyone; everybody sees through you. When the team members see your weaknesses, they start attacking them. The more they attack, the more you cover up, the more obvious it becomes. This is not good.

The way to overcome your insecurities is not by trying to hide them but by being humble enough to admit what they are. Instead of trying to shield them, present them. Ask for some help. Explain your shortfalls and what you want to do to correct them.

You do have to be careful not to go overboard. Being humble does not mean you should present yourself as incompetent. You should prepare and do enough research to understand your areas of weakness. If a new blind spot is uncovered, take notes and figure out the best way to reinforce the area where you are lacking.

This is an important concept to understand; humility and vulnerability can work together to make you better. If you are humble enough to admit when you have a vulnerability, you can then address it, reinforce it, and get it solved. This is contrary to the intuitive idea of hiding or masking your weaknesses. That does not work. The true way to overcome your insecurities is to admit them to yourself, air them to the team, and then work to improve them.

TRANSITIONING FROM FOLLOWER OR PEER TO LEADER

There are times in many organizations when an individual must be elevated from a peer group into a leadership position. This can be a difficult transition. Obviously, there are close relationships among peers that would not normally develop in a leader-to-subordinate situation

I got to witness this type of transition in two of my SEAL platoons. In each case, one of the "boys"—one of the young enlisted SEALs troopers—was selected to step up and become the LPO, or leading petty officer, of the platoon. The way SEAL platoons were structured at that time, the LPO was the fourth in command. There would be an officer in charge (OIC), an assistant officer in charge (AOIC), a platoon chief (CPO), and finally the LPO.

LPOs would usually have more experience than the rest of the SEALs in the platoon but would not necessarily be senior to them in rank. Nonetheless, it was a position of authority, and the LPO was the individual who transferred much of the commander's intent from the OIC and CPO to the troops and actually made things happen.

Both of the times one of my peers was elevated to LPO in my SEAL platoons, the circumstances were similar. The platoons had just been formed up, but no LPO had been assigned. Each time, we were wondering who our LPO would be. Often, LPOs would come from another team or a training command (which was done to mitigate preexisting excessive familiarity between the LPO and the troops).

The first time it happened, we junior enlisted SEALs were sitting in our platoon hut talking when the OIC and CPO came in. They called out one of the SEALs who was more experienced than the rest of us, but who was of the same rank and who was still "one of the boys." I'll call him Larry. The OIC and the CPO asked Larry to go with them, and they told the rest of us to stand by.

So we stood by and waited.

What we didn't know was that Larry was taken to see the commanding officer and command master chief of the SEAL Team, where he was told he had been selected to serve as the LPO of our platoon.

About a half hour went by, and then Larry returned with the OIC and CPO.

"Listen up, gents," the CPO said. "Larry has been selected to be the LPO of this platoon. He will be running you guys from now on. Give him the support he deserves."

"Roger that, Chief," we said.

With that, Larry pulled out what we called a *wheel book*—a simple, navy-issued, four-by-six notebook—and started looking at a checklist of things that needed to get done.

"All right, fellas. As you heard from Chief, I'm the LPO now. It's an honor. Now, here's what we still need to get done today. First, we have a full weapons and sensitive items inventory to do, including radios, night vision, and crypto. Once that is done, we need all gear staged by 1000 on the grinder so we can get pallets built for the next trip. Of course, that means hazardous material paperwork needs to get turned so lithium batteries, fuel, and ordnance can be shipped. I want to get those pallets built by lunch so we can do some walk-throughs of our immediate action drills this afternoon. We will start those at 1300. Once we hammer out some of those, I want to wrap up the day by 1430 or 1500 so you all get some time at home before we leave. What do you guys think? Did I miss anything?"

Larry had quickly (in just about thirty minutes!) stepped up into the LPO position and taken charge. He was respectful and appreciative, but at the same time confident. He gave us clear guidance and direction. It was just what we needed. We got busy and got things done, just as we would continue to get things done for Larry and for the platoon. It worked well.

Interestingly, in my very next platoon, about eighteen months later, another one of my peers was elevated to the position of LPO. We had just formed up and were once again sitting around in our platoon space wondering who our LPO was going to be. It was odd to be in a platoon with no LPO assigned, since the LPO is a critical part of the leadership team. But it had happened, and once again, one of the enlisted SEAL shooters was summoned by the OIC and CPO. Once again, he was brought to meet with the commanding officer and command master chief and told he was taking over as the LPO. And once again, this individual, whom I will call Brian, was brought back down and introduced to us as our new LPO.

But this time, when he came back, it was different. Instead of pulling out a wheel book with a checklist and telling us what needed to be done, instead of giving us a schedule with some deadlines, instead of asking us what we thought, he just cracked a joke, saying, "Looks like I'm responsible for all the crap now." That was it. That was the word he had to put out. That was how he tried to take the reins as LPO. It was completely ineffective.

It should be noted that Brian was a great guy and a great SEAL operator, but he wasn't quite ready to make the transition to leadership. So as a platoon, we floundered for a few months until he got his leadership bearings and started to run things properly.

But that isn't necessary; there is no reason to flounder. When you transition from within a group to becoming a leader of that group, you have to step up. This doesn't mean you have to know everything. This doesn't mean you need to lay down the law. But it does mean you have to differentiate who you were as one of the troops from who you are now as a leader.

- *Come up with a plan.*
- *Give simple, clear, concise direction.*
- *Stay humble, take input, and listen.*
- *And, of course, lead.*

There is one final point to mention. Once you move into a leadership position, you have to step not only up but also out of the weeds. You will have to stop doing some of the old things you are used to doing—things you are comfortable doing—and start doing things that you aren't so comfortable with.

As a leader, your goal should be to look up and out, not down and in at your team. So when transitioning to a leadership position, the goal is not only to guide the development of the plan but then also to oversee its execution. This means the leader should not be doing much of the actual doing. Let the troops do the doing. If the leader is doing, he or she isn't leading. The leader who is doing is looking down and in at the team instead of up and out at the future. So let the troops do.

Of course, there is a dichotomy to balance. This does not mean the leader is above hard work. The leader must not become detached to a point where they are aloof from what is happening and what the frontline troops have to contend with.

Don't be the leader with your hands in your pockets, but don't be the leader with your hands in everything.

OVERCOMING A GRUDGE

There will be times in your career when you will be the one promoted into a leadership position and placed above your former peers. This can be challenging, but when handled correctly, the challenge can be mitigated. Most of your former peers will accept the situation and get on board. But sometimes there are people who get bitter and resentful that they weren't promoted, and they show that bitterness.

There are some ways to mitigate a bad attitude from your former peers. First off, don't try to force your rank down their throats. Tell them you appreciate their experience and you will be looking to them to help lead the team. Let them come up with plans and ideas. Ask for and listen to their input. If they come up with a solid plan, let them run with it.

When the opportunity arises, put them in charge of some tasks, projects, and missions. This shows them that you trust them and truly do appreciate their experience and knowledge, and if they can put their egos in check, the situation can be overcome.

But also be advised that some people will be hypersensitive and see you putting them in charge of something as condescending, or as proof that you don't know what you are doing and that they should have been promoted, not you. When their pouting and bad attitude become apparent, recognize that the likely reason they were not promoted (assuming they do have the most knowledge and experience) is because they likely lack the humility and maturity to be a leader. If that is the case, continue to be cordial, treat them with respect, and try to build a relationship with them, but don't expect rapid improvement from them. This will be a long process; you are going to have to be patient and make sure you don't let them distract you from the mission or the rest of the team.

NEW SHERIFF IN TOWN

There is a broad spectrum of approaches to take when implementing change after moving into a leadership position inside a team or organization. One method is to come in hard and immediately start making changes and imposing one's will on the team. The opposite end of the spectrum is spending a large amount of time observing, then slowly making changes in an incremental manner. In between these two extremes are many other methodologies that can be utilized. Which methodology should a leader use when taking over a team?

The answer depends on the situation the leader is going into. It is a good idea to know as much as possible about the mission and the troops before even taking over. Request to review documents that explain day-to-day operations, describe the nature of the work, and expound on how it gets done. Obviously, a thorough turnover from the previous leader of the team is ideal. Talking through the state of the team, gaining understanding of the challenges it is presented with, and getting feedback on the personalities involved, as well as their various strengths and weaknesses, is beneficial in getting up to speed.

When receiving information from the departing boss, it is important to remember where they are coming from and what is influencing their perspective. Are they being fired? Do they have personal relationships with members of the team? Do they have a big ego that might attempt to undermine the new leader? Whatever the situation, it is important to understand the bias or spin an outgoing leader might be putting on their turnover.

In addition to reading documents pertinent to the team's mission and discussing the job with the departing boss, a new leader should try to know the people on the team to the best of his or her ability before he or she even meets them. How does a leader do that? A simple way is to review records; find out what training they have been through on an individual and collective level. Request and study in advance a guidebook that has a picture of every member of the team and that explains their positions, skills, experience, some of their personal interests, and their family situations.

The new leader must also consider the status of the team he is taking over. It might be a high-performing organization or a failing team. But organizations seldom fall neatly into these extreme categories. Most will be somewhere in between; therefore, the approach must be modulated and balanced to accommodate the situation the leader is entering.

So be smart. Don't change things that are working, but don't accept things that are not working. The better the team is, the less you have to change. The worse it is, the more will need adjusting.

It is easy to see some of the methods used when applied to the extreme examples. If I am taking over a team that is squared away, has a great attitude, and is accomplishing the mission, I am going to go in fairly gently. I am going to introduce myself and make myself available, but I am obviously not going to go in barking orders and imposing my way on the team members. They are already functioning well. They have good relationships. They are succeeding. I am not going to interfere with an organization that is doing well. I will simply observe closely, learn all I can about how they work, and eventually see if there are any areas where some level of improvement is possible. The old saying "If it ain't broke, don't fix it" is a wise assessment. If a team is working well, I am not going to try to fix it.

Once actually on board with a new team that is performing well, take the opportunity to get to know the team. If time and logistics allow it, schedule a formal meeting with the whole team and then schedule meetings with individual team members. But don't only interact on an official level, visit with the team members informally as they perform their functions, drop in on some meetings, and walk the grounds getting to know team members and what they do. This is a time to build relationships that will become the basis of trust and camaraderie that are the foundation of any team.

Contrarily, if I am joining a failing team that is having significant problems and I am aware of the cause of those problems, I am going to take a more direct approach and be aggressive. I will research what the problems are, and I will bring a couple of ideas to implement immediately. I will lay out a clear vision and new mission, and I will emphasize some specific things that are going to change. I will set in place some new processes, move personnel to different roles, and perhaps even terminate some people who are causing significant problems. There will be no doubt in anyone's mind that the status quo is gone.

If I am joining a team that has significant problems, but I don't have a clear comprehension of what the problems are, I will still make some changes, but the changes will not have an impact on current operations. I will change communication protocol; change, add, or subtract meeting times; and perhaps implement a new dress code or make other fairly benign adjustments that get the attention of the team but don't interfere with anything. I will try to develop a relationship with some of the senior leadership team, some of the midlevel managers, and the frontline troops, interviewing them all separately as I try to get a feel for the ground truth. I will ask a lot of questions and get to know the personnel as I look for trusted agents at every level. I will be slow to open that trust since a failing team is such a traumatic experience, and those suffering through it can be emotional and make false and misleading statements about the situation and other people in it. In these situations, take everything with a grain of salt.

Once I start isolating the problem areas and deducing what the issues might be, I will incrementally make more impactful changes, slowly but surely, as I get feedback and understand their effects on the situation.

The better the team members, the more I will lean on them to come up with solutions in areas where improvement is needed. Ideally, I simply identify problem areas, and they come up with solutions for them. In doing that, they take ownership and execute. However, if the team is grossly subpar, I will certainly listen to the members' input, but I will do so more critically, as their track record indicates a lack of ability to identify and solve problems.

I also have to pay close attention to the fact that the leader I am replacing might have been the cause of many of the problems within the team. When the bad leader is replaced, sometimes the subordinates are ready to step up and make things happen. There is a chance that once the team members are unburdened from their bad leader, they will begin to perform exceptionally. I need to make sure I do not hinder that.

So once I have established some relationships and sense of understanding with a high-performing team, I will start to make incremental changes until they reach maximum efficiency. For a low-performing team, I will do the opposite: start off with dramatic changes and back off over time as things begin to function properly. Again, depending on the progress of the team members and their actual performance, I will have to modulate my leadership methods with them, adjusting my level of guidance, interaction, and direction based on what they do.

DON'T GO OVERBOARD, RAMBO

You want to be a leader. That's great. But don't be offensive about it. What does that mean? It means don't run around saying, "I'm the leader! I am in charge! Listen to me! I'll make the decisions!" This attitude will offend many people. It is the equivalent of "Look at me! I'm important!" and it doesn't go over well. Rambo might be a cool movie character, but charging out alone without regard for others doesn't work in a team environment. Saying, "I am the leader; follow me!" can offend people's egos. In their minds, perhaps they are thinking you don't deserve to be in charge. There is a good chance they are even thinking that they are the one who should be in charge. So you barking at them that you are the leader is not a good idea. And when you do make some kind of mistake—which you will—they will be ready to pounce on it.

Leadership, in most cases, should be subtle. Of course, there are situations where bold and overt leadership is needed. If there is an emergency and no one is taking action, it is time to step up and take charge. If morale is down, the troops are stagnating, and movement is needed, it is time to lead from the front. But in everyday situations, overt leadership is not needed. It is better to give subtle direction and let the troops move forward based on their own ideas.

The same thing goes for mentoring and coaching. If you are looking to mentor or coach someone, be subtle about it. Many people might say they want to be coached or mentored but have a hard time when someone actually steps up to do it. Because let's face it, there is an implicit message when you offer to coach or mentor someone—you are implying not only that the other person is lacking in some areas but also that you are better than they are! That can really bother people, especially if they have big egos. Unfortunately, the people with the biggest egos are usually the ones who need the most coaching.

So instead of outright telling someone you are going to lead, coach, or mentor them, be subtler:

- *Instead of, "I'll tell you how we are going to execute," try, "How do you think we should execute?"*
- *Instead of, "Let me coach you how to do that," try, "Can you explain why you do it that way?"*
- *Instead of, "I will mentor you," try, "I would love to compare how you do things to how I do them."*

The latter options of these statements are indirect approaches. What they are really doing is starting a conversation, opening the door to discussion, and disarming any defenses that might be activated by a direct approach. Once the discussion is started, you can contribute your thoughts and ideas by embedding them into the conversation. If your methods, techniques, and plans are superior, that should be apparent, and the person you are trying to coach will be more receptive to your ideas. Over time, you can then indirectly sway the individual toward your way of thinking in a way that will be much more acceptable to them than if you shove your mentorship or coaching down their throat.

Occasionally, you may encounter a person who craves your leadership and truly desires to be mentored. When that happens, of course, you can be more direct and straightforward. But even in those situations, be careful. Sometimes when people are asking for criticism, they can still be offended when you give it to them. So use caution and always start with a softer approach.

The people who taught me the most about leadership, strategy, and tactics never explicitly told me they were coaching or mentoring me; they subtly guided me along the path, filling my head with knowledge, while I barely even noticed it. They managed to teach me without teaching me, putting ideas into my brain so delicately that I thought the ideas were my own. That is the most powerful way to teach, coach, and mentor.

When I think back to the best leaders I ever worked for, they were also incredibly subtle. Very rarely did they come right out and give direct orders stating exactly what to do and how to do it. The best leaders usually led not by orders but by suggestion. As often as they could, they put their ideas out there and allowed us, the troops, to identify those ideas as the best and then move toward enacting their ideas through our own volition. This is an incredibly powerful way to lead—perhaps the most powerful. It instills an incredible level of ownership into the troops because they all get the feeling that the ideas they are executing are actually their own. Indirect leadership almost always trumps direct leadership.

But notice that I said *almost*. There are also times when direct leadership is needed, usually during times of duress, where critical and immediate decisions must be made. During those times, a leader stepping up and making a call is not only preferred, it is required. The same thing can happen during moments of indecision. If a team can't decide which way to go—if multiple ideas are being batted around and argued about—that is another time when a leader might need to step up and make a decision.

In all these cases, because the leader has been restrained from constantly making decisions for the group, when he or she does step in and make a call, it will be respected. That is a stark contrast to the leader who constantly feels the need to make every decision, to drive every choice, and be at the center of all conversations and conclusions. That leader's voice loses value because it is heard too often.

So don't go overboard. Not as a leader, not as a mentor, and not as a coach. Don't be Rambo. Instead, be as subtle as you can—until you can't. And then *lead*.

LEADERSHIP SKILLS

WHEN TO STEP UP AND LEAD

There is a dichotomy between when to lead and when to follow. Even if you are in charge, if there is someone with a good plan who is giving direction to move the right way, that's fine; take a step back and let them lead. Be a follower.

There are times when a leadership vacuum occurs—no one is taking charge of a situation. Bad circumstances are unfolding, but no one is doing anything about it. No one is leading.

That is a moment where someone needs to jump in and take charge; you will see that people are waiting for it. They are waiting for leadership, and when you step up with a simple plan and give clear direction, they will accept that direction and execute.

But it isn't always that simple. If you are the only one who has recognized the threat of inaction, if you are the only one who recognizes the leadership void, then other people on the team might not be waiting for someone to start leading. They might think everything is okay.

So if you jump up and start barking orders, they might be taken aback by it; they might be offended or feel you are stepping on their toes.

That's why you might want to hesitate a moment when you see that leadership vacuum appear. That is a tactic that I used as a leader throughout my career. Of course, if there was an immediate threat that needed to be addressed instantaneously and no one was doing anything, I would step up immediately and make a call; I would fill the leadership void.

However, if there was a problem unfolding a little more slowly, I wouldn't rush to take charge; I would let the problem develop a little bit. I would look around, detach mentally, and truly observe the situation. I would confirm that what I was seeing was correct. I would allow an opportunity for someone else to step up and fill the leadership vacuum—and if someone else did, then I would internally assess their plan and the directions they were giving. If they were giving good guidance, I would support them. If they gave bad guidance, I would continue to consider what a better plan was so I could give corrections when the time was right.

When someone else wouldn't step up quickly, it was usually because no one else had noticed there was a leadership vacuum. They wouldn't notice because they were not detached; their minds were absorbed in the situation. Since I practiced being detached, I wasn't lost in the details of what was going on. I was mentally in a different place, looking at a scenario unfold from a virtual distance, which allowed me to see problems more quickly.

That still doesn't mean I would jump right in. By letting a little more time pass, by letting that leadership void linger just a little bit longer, everyone else would begin to notice it; they would recognize there was a problem. Since that time passed and now everyone else knew there was a problem, when I gave orders on how to solve it, people would listen, and they would execute.

Another reason to pause before jumping into a leadership vacuum as soon as you see it is to make sure that no one else is jumping in there. If two people step in to fill a leadership void at the same time, they usually bump into each other when they get there. Then, while the problem they are trying to solve grows, they have to take precious time to sort out which person is going to actually lead and which one is going to stand down. If egos clash at this moment, it is going to be problematic.

I would rather avoid that. If someone else is going to step in with a plan, that is fine with me. So when I see the void, I pause, look around, and assess if anyone else is going to step up and lead. While I do this, the problem grows. Soon everyone notices the problem. I see that, and then I step in and make a call, a call that everyone knows needs to be made, a call that everyone is waiting for. That means when I spoke, people listened.

There is one more advantage gained by taking a tactical pause before jumping into a leadership vacuum: by giving those last few moments to allow things to develop, the call you make will be better. That pause allows you to understand the problem and the solution more clearly, and the direction you give will be on point. This means people will follow your lead.

There is also an inverse to the leadership vacuum, which is when too many people try to lead. Everyone wants to offer their opinion, give advice, and weigh in on the decision. This can inhibit the decision-making process and the leader's ability to lead.

A similar thing happens on the battlefield—troops bunch up in tight groups. This is not good, because if soldiers are bunched up, one well-placed round—or simply a lucky one—can kill or wound many of the people clustered. That can be any kind of round: a bullet, a mortar round, a rocket-propelled grenade, or even an improvised explosive device.

To prevent this, we in the military are taught *dispersion*. Dispersion simply means *spread out,* to get some space between you and the other members of your team. "Don't bunch up," was a common critique to platoons bogged down in a training evolution. Now, this may seem simple, but it can be difficult, as there are some compelling forces that draw people together.

The first force is psychological safety. When we get scared, having another person nearby can be comforting. Since most people are looking for that psychological comfort, even subconsciously, it doesn't take long before three, four, or five people have congregated in hopes of finding some relief. As soon as a group gets that big, its members are bunched up and at risk.

Another force that tends to make people converge on one another is opportunity. There are usually limited areas that provide cover and concealment, and since cover and concealment provide safety and security, most of the troops will want to be in those areas. That means those areas will be crowded, and once again, the troops will be bunched up

One last influence that tends to draw people into closer range of one another is the desire to know what is going on, to see and hear what is happening, and to communicate with other people on the team. This means when one person stops, people tend to flock around them so they can talk face-to-face.

So there are a lot of forces at work on teams in the field that cause them to gather like a flock waiting to be slaughtered by one bullet or one bomb. It is only through the understanding of that tendency and repetitive training that the natural instinct for people to bunch up can be overcome.

But the phrase *Don't bunch up* can just as easily be applied to leadership. Many people have the tendency to crowd around the leader, to invade their mental real estate and step on their toes, undermining the leader's authority and denigrating the capability of the team by interfering with the leader. Bunching up on the leader hurts the team.

The main thing that causes us to want to bunch up around and interfere with the leader in a situation is our egos. Many people have an intrinsic desire to be in charge. We want to make decisions. We want to be important. When we aren't the ones in charge, our egos hurt. To prop up our egos, we start trying to infringe on the actual leader and prove that *we* are the ones who should be making the decisions.

We also often think our ideas are the best possible ideas. Once again, that is just our egos talking. Instead of listening, we talk. Instead of allowing a leader the time and space to make a decision, we bombard them with our own ideas. Instead of supporting the leader, we bump into them and cause disruption.

Even when our egos are in check, we still have the desire to contribute and help the cause. That can translate into us forcing our ideas into the mix, which is not useful in a situation where execution is needed more than ideas.

So step away. Don't crowd the leader by trying to finagle your own ideas and plans into the mix. It does not help. Instead, give the leader room to lead. Don't bunch up.

DON'T TAKE THINGS PERSONALLY

This may seem obvious, but I see all the time where people take things personally. Don't take anything personally. It is hard to do this. You have to fight your ego to avoid taking things personally. Even when people ask for critique points, they often get mad when they actually hear them. Don't allow yourself to do that. Don't take criticism personally.

Not about the plan you came up with.

Not about the idea you had.

Not about the presentation you gave.

Not about the decision you made.

Even when your biggest rival, the last person you want to hear from, has something to say, listen.

Even when someone you don't think is on your level, someone who isn't even close to having the knowledge, position, or authority to give you one iota of feedback wants to speak, even then, do yourself a favor and just listen. Detach and listen to what they have to say and, from an objective mind-set, see if you can learn anything at all from their commentary. Then apply it. And say thank you. I know that stings. Get over yourself.

This takes humility, but it will make you better.

DON'T DIG IN

General George S. Patton famously told his troops not to dig in; he wanted them to advance, advance, and advance. You can't advance if you are dug in.

Patton's idea of not digging in actually translates incredibly well from a leadership perspective, and it is one that I always kept in the back of my mind. When you have an idea, thought, or opinion, don't dig in. That means *don't overcommit to ideas.* Keep an open mind, and leave yourself an out.

When I was in a leadership position in the SEAL Teams, there were always lots of different ideas floating around. How to execute a mission. What plan to use. Which tactics were best. And like many organizations, no one could ever seem to agree on anything; but it was always safe to assume that when different people had different ideas, the idea that people liked the best was almost always *their own.* Maybe it is ego, maybe it is pride, or maybe it is just that people can see their own perspective better than anyone else's. This is not unique to the SEAL Teams. People in different organizations everywhere all do the same thing; they tend to think their idea is the best, and then they get hung up arguing about it.

Arguing is generally bad. It means wasting time without moving forward—and what is worse, people often argue not for *the best* idea but for *their idea.* What really makes for a horrible situation is when people not only think their idea is the best but they *dig in* to protect it. They aren't going to give any ground. They cannot concede a single inch in admitting theirs is not the best idea of all time. The more they come under attack, the deeper they dig in—they will not change their minds. To translate this back to tactical terms, when people dig in to defend their ideas, not only can they not advance them, they also cannot maneuver and change their thoughts. They are dug in, and they can't move.

I used to see this all the time with some leaders inside a SEAL platoon. They would come up with their idea or plan and then dig in and defend it with zero compromise. It was awful to see—hours of fruitless arguments, which were not ever driving toward the best solution but driving toward the leader's own solution. Leaders often painted themselves into corners so that eventually they would be left with no choice except to order their subordinates to follow their plan.

If the person who had dug in was not the boss but a subordinate, eventually their boss would just order them to go in a different direction, which they would then do, begrudgingly, after wasting hours of time and energy.

I always avoided this. I would seldom dig in and get overcommitted to my idea, my plan, or my opinion. When someone had an opposing point of view, I didn't look for ways to prove my idea was better; instead, I looked to see which idea was *actually* better. If my idea wasn't as good, I conceded and accepted theirs. If the ideas were relatively equal, I would defer to theirs so they had ownership. If my idea was far superior, then the differences were usually obvious enough to convince the person with the opposing view that they were wrong—and I would never have to admit that I was wrong, because I never claimed that I was right.

There were rare occasions when I actually would dig in. One of those occasions would be if I knew with 100 percent certainty that I was right. Since it is almost impossible to know something with 100 percent certainty, this almost never happened. I would also dig in if the subject dealt with immoral, illegal, or unethical activities.

Finally, if someone wanted to violate the fundamental Laws of Combat that I knew to be true, I would hold my ground. And even in these cases, I would almost always try to leave myself some room to maneuver (see page 56 on mutinies) since it is almost never good to get yourself in a position or situation you can't get out of.

Don't dig in unless you have no choice—and, even then, always try to leave yourself some room to maneuver.

Of course, while not digging in is usually great advice, from a tactical perspective, if you get bogged down on the battlefield and can't move or if you decide to hold fast in one position, you should absolutely *dig in*. If you stagnate on the battlefield—if you cannot move for whatever reason—then you should fortify your position. This also applies to leadership; if you are faced with a rare situation where you must defend yourself, then make sure you can solidly defend your position.

ITERATIVE DECISION-MAKING

"Be decisive!" leaders are often told. I know I heard many SEAL leaders reprimanded because they weren't making decisions fast enough. Sometimes, it was me doing the reprimanding. In many cases, that is great advice. Indecision can make horrible situations worse. In the SEAL Teams, indecision is commonly called *analysis paralysis.* That means a leader is overwhelmed by the events unfolding around them and can't decide what to do. It can occur in any leadership environment, and it is not good. If you aren't maneuvering, the enemy is, and allowing the enemy to maneuver is one way to allow them to get the upper hand.

Of course, rushing to make a decision without fully understanding what is happening can be just as bad. An obvious example is receiving a small amount of enemy fire and making the decision to attack immediately. If you haven't let the situation develop, it could turn out that small amount of enemy fire might have simply been bait to lure your team into a channelized kill zone and wipe you all out. Making a rash call is clearly not the right thing to do in that situation.

As a leader, you have to learn to let situations develop, to allow things to unfold enough that you have a clear picture of what is happening. Until you have a relatively good idea of what is going on, it is foolish to make a conclusive decision about what you and your team should do.

But that doesn't mean you shouldn't make any decision at all. In times like this, when I've been unsure about a situation or did not have good enough information to make a bold, clear decision, I utilized an iterative decision-making process. That means I looked at the situation and made small decisions to move toward a direction that aligned with my best guess on what the situation was, without overcommitting since I wasn't sure.

As an example, let's say your platoon is tasked with assaulting a building where an insurgent is suspected to be bedding down for the night. This insurgent has been on the move for several months, and this is the first time his location has been predicted. The target building where he is suspected of being is located three hundred miles from your location. Because of possible surface-to-air missiles protecting the target building, you are told not to utilize helicopters to get to it. This means you and your platoon have to drive to the target building—approximately five hours to get there and five hours to get back. It will also take a couple of hours to do a final reconnaissance of the target building and to clear it. So to complete the whole mission in one cycle of darkness, darkness that gives you stealth and an advantage over the enemy since you have night vision capability, you need to leave just after sunset to ensure you have time to drive to the target, hit it, and return to base before sunrise.

One major problem is that you aren't sure the insurgent is in the building; he is only *suspected* of being there. But you have to remember that when your troops are out on the roads driving, they are under the threat of being hit by an enemy improvised explosive device or ambush. That is a big risk for a mere suspicion, so you should not immediately commit to taking down the target. Instead, you should just have the platoon start their planning process, which will take several hours. You would also tell them to include several stops along the way at friendly forward operating bases, where they will be able to better assess the target when they are planning routes.

Just before sunset, your platoon will brief the plan and check the intelligence department for information about the insurgent's location. If he is still suspected of being in the target building tonight, you will proceed, but not yet all the way to the target. Instead, you will proceed to a forward operating base that is two hundred miles from the target. Once there, you check the intelligence again and see where the suspect is. You still haven't fully committed to executing the mission, but if the intelligence indicates the suspect is still going to be bedding down in the target location, you will continue on. And you will do this again at one hundred miles and again at the last forward operating base, only twelve miles from the target. If at any point intelligence reveals that the insurgent is not going to be at the target building, you can pause, assess, and turn back. By doing this, you mitigate how much risk you are taking with the safety of your troops and how much risk you take in burning the target, which means making the enemy aware that the location is not safe for him.

After all, if you hit the target and the enemy isn't there, then there is almost zero chance he will return to that location, and you will miss the chance of capturing him there in the future. But by making the decision in smaller, iterative steps that move toward the goal, you can reduce the chances of that happening.

The idea of iterative decision-making is contrary to the idea of being decisive, but if you had heard about the target and immediately and decisively ordered your team to launch and hit it, there is no telling how bad that might have been. You would have put your men at risk of enemy attack during six hundred miles of driving, and you would have risked burning the target for follow-on operations.

So be decisive when you need to be, but try not to make decisions until you have to. Assess what is happening to the best of your ability with the information you have, and then make smaller decisions with minimum commitment to move in the direction you most highly suspect is the right one.

DECENTRALIZED COMMAND OR LAZY DESIGNATION?

Decentralized Command requires that leaders push tasks and authorities down to their subordinate leaders, who in turn push those tasks and authorities to the frontline leaders and troops. In fact, I often say that if a leader wants to be in charge of everything, then he or she should try to be in charge of nothing. Only when a leader is in charge of nothing, when he or she has delegated all actions to his or her subordinate leaders, can the leader truly lead. It is impossible to lead a team forward in a strategic direction when you are busy trying to direct and manage less significant tasks that could be handled by subordinates, so it is imperative that a leader utilize Decentralized Command and let his or her subordinate leaders lead.

But as a leader delegates tasks, projects, and authorities to his or her subordinate leaders, it can seem that the boss doesn't want to do anything at all. At what point do the troops start thinking the boss is lazy or that the boss doesn't want to take responsibility for hard tasks, missions, or projects?

This can be a real problem, but there are some simple ways to prevent it. First, if you sense any inkling of attitude from the troops that you are shying away from the tough missions or tasks, then take charge of the most challenging ones and crush them. Set the example. Lead from the front.

The same thing applies if you hear actual complaints from your subordinates about being assigned a particular task. If that happens, simply take over the assignment and get it done. "Oh, you don't want to do that? Okay. I will."

It shouldn't take long for the complainers to realize that if they turn over their work to you, they will be out of a job. It also often hits their own egos; as they give up a task to you, they lose control over it, they give up ownership, and, in doing so, they give you more ownership. That can sting, and it can change their attitudes.

But sometimes their attitudes don't change. There is a possibility that they will simply allow you to take over jobs from them because they don't want to do them. Perhaps the complainer is lazy. Perhaps they don't mind giving up ownership because they don't want any. Perhaps they don't feel any impact to their ego because they don't have any pride in their work—they don't care. If this is the reaction you get from a team member, good; it is a clear indication that they don't want to do their job and are not invested in their own performance, and you should start looking for options to remove them from their position.

The final thing to do to prevent giving your troops the impression that your delegation is avoidance of hard work is to take on some of the harshest jobs yourself. Do some of the nasty work. Get down in the grime, get your hands dirty, and get the most awful job done. This shouldn't be a task that takes a lot of time; you don't want it to encroach on the critical time you need to be looking up and out. Obviously, you cannot spend all your time on these types of tasks, but showing that you are more than willing to do them will remove any thought from the minds of your team members that you are delegating to avoid work. It will also clearly display your humility, which will increase their respect for you.

THE EASY BUTTON

Taking ownership, especially of hard tasks, does not mean doing everything for your team or your subordinate leaders. If you do that too much, you run the risk of becoming the "easy button" for them.

What does that mean? It means whenever there is a problem with even the slightest level of difficulty, the team members will want you to solve it for them. You make their jobs and their lives easy by doing this.

While occasionally stepping in and problem solving is required of a leader, if it becomes your default mode, and if the troops begin to expect it, then it will ultimately hurt the team because you will constantly be looking down and in instead of up and out. You will be focused on tactical-level issues when you should be looking at the strategic picture and figuring out what the next move will be.

Worse, though, is that you will stunt the collective growth and progression of the team and the individuals that make it up. They will not learn to think; they will only learn to ask you for solutions. This will halt their progress and development as leaders themselves.

When I was a task unit commander, I had the most experience of the officers in our unit. I had not only taught every aspect of SEAL advanced training as an enlisted SEAL, I had also done six overseas deployments, including one as a SEAL platoon commander in Iraq conducting scores of direct-action missions targeting enemy personnel. The other officers in the task unit had only done a fraction of those types of missions, so my understanding of how to plan and execute direct-action missions was above and beyond what my junior officers understood. They knew this, so when we were going through our training cycle preparing for deployment and needed to plan a training mission, my officers would often come to me and ask how they should do it.

Of course, the first few times they asked me, I gave them some ideas and guidance based on lessons I had learned. But it didn't take long before I began telling them, "Go figure it out yourself and come back to me when you think you have a good plan." At first, they were nervous while presenting their plans to me, perhaps thinking I might jump down their throats and chew them out for their poor planning. But they soon realized I wasn't looking to scold or abuse them; I was looking to teach and train them. As they presented their plans to me, I would counsel them on their shortfalls and point out elements that were tactically unsound. They would then correct those parts and come back with better plans. Over time, after planning dozens of operations during our training cycle, they had a solid understanding of how to plan missions. By the time we got overseas, I didn't have to worry about their plans anymore because they could plan as well as or better than I could. That allowed me to focus on looking at the overall operational picture, deconflicting with other friendly units, and making sure we were properly supporting the overall objectives of our higher headquarters.

I was able to lead because the guys below me learned how to do their jobs and mine. That allowed me to look up and out instead of down and in. Don't stunt the growth of your team members. Don't solve every problem they come to you with. Don't be the easy button.

JUDGING REPUTATIONS

As a leader, you will constantly be introduced to new people, whether you are taking over a team, a new member is joining your team, or you are going to be working with individuals from another team. No matter which case, the individuals you are introduced to will have reputations. Their history will precede them. They will usually have some kind of a written (or virtual) record of evaluations, including previous performance, awards, and punitive actions they might have received.

As a new leader, don't judge them based on what you have heard or read; try to keep an open mind and judge for yourself. This isn't to say you should not consider any prior history that a person might have; read it, listen to it, make note of it. But give the person the benefit of a fresh start.

Since you have noted and studied their past performance, you can make a quicker assessment about what you see. If you know a person has a history of being late and they show up late for work, you instantly know it is a real problem. If a person has a history of getting emotional and you see them getting emotional, they have confirmed the problem.

But if someone shows up with some negative facts on their résumé or record, give them a chance. Their last boss might have been a nightmare. They might not have had the experience to do the job and fell short. They might have made some immature mistakes. All these problems can likely be resolved and overcome if a person is given a chance and if that person is led properly. Do your job and *lead*.

CONFORM TO INFLUENCE

As a leader, I always liked when I had people on my team who were highly motivated, aggressive, and fired up to get the job done. I much prefer someone I have to reel in over someone I need to push. It wasn't only when I was a leader that I liked that. Even as a junior member of the team, I always loved when the other members were ready to get after it.

But that isn't always the case. Not everyone likes to get after it. In fact, being fired up can actually offend people up and down the chain of command. How is that? It usually has to do with ego, but there are other reasons as well. I learned about this in my very first SEAL platoon as a new guy.

As a new guy, I was extremely motivated. I wanted to train as hard as possible to prepare for war. But this was 1992, and there was no war happening. The first Gulf War had ended six months earlier and had lasted only seventy-two hours. The Vietnam War, where SEALs had earned the fierce reputation that made me want to be a SEAL, had ended twenty years earlier. This was a full-on peacetime navy.

But I was young and figured my war was coming, so I wanted to be ready for it. So I did things a little bit differently from most other people at SEAL Team One. I got to work early. I did our team conditioning runs with heavy boots on instead of running shoes. I wore a rucksack with a forty-pound sandbag in it when we ran the obstacle course. I did night ocean swims alone with my web gear on. I tried to do everything just a little bit harder than what was normally required. I thought it was the right thing to do—after all, *I was preparing for war!*

Unfortunately, my attitude was not appreciated by some of the older guys in my platoon. Sure, the other new guys who knew me understood my attitude because they went through BUD/S with me; they knew I was just fired up. But some of the older guys thought I was going overboard. For them, after having been in the SEAL Teams for six, eight, ten, or even a dozen years, they knew that sustained performance as a SEAL wasn't a sprint, it was a marathon. They knew that additional wear and tear on the knees, shoulders, ankles, and back had to be monitored and mitigated. They knew we were about to start an extensive and arduous workup of long patrols, parachuting, fast-roping, diving, and all kinds of other evolutions that would put intense physical demands on all of us. Those physical demands would be even harder on guys who had already done multiple workups and deployments. But for us new guys coming straight out of BUD/S, we were healthy and ready to charge, and in my mind I was personally trying to take it to the next level.

It didn't take long before I started to hear grumbling from some of those more experienced guys. Little comments started to let me know they weren't seeing things quite the same way I was. "Here comes Rambo," or "Look at this tough guy." At first, they sounded like they were joking. But the tone got stronger, and before long I realized they did not like what I was doing.

Now, it could have been very easy for me to assess the situation and cast blame on *them*. I could have said to myself, *What is wrong with them? I'm the one who is working extra hard. They are being weak. I'm hardcore—much more hardcore than they are. I am preparing for* war! *These guys should be working hard to be ready for combat like I am. In fact, can I even rely on these guys?*

As a young SEAL, still teeming with confidence after completing "the world's hardest military training," I could easily rationalize my own behavior and at the same time denigrate the other members of my platoon. Especially because in my platoon, some of the older guys weren't in the best physical condition. *Of course they don't want to do extra physical activity! They are weak, and I am strong. They must be intimidated by me! Their egos are too big to handle a new guy like me coming in and getting after it!*

But then I thought about it from their perspective. *Who am I? I am a new guy. I have never been on deployment before.* I had never been through a workup before. Who was I to judge them? What did I know?

Then I thought about it from a team perspective. *We are a platoon; we are supposed to be a team, to work together.* And here I was, alienating myself from the team. There was a rift forming between some of the older guys in the platoon and me. That was wrong. It was disrupting the unity of the platoon, which negatively impacted our operational readiness.

So you know what I did? I backed off. I did extra work on my own time, but when I was with the platoon, I tried to act like the rest of the guys. To put it bluntly, I *conformed.*

That is something that no one wants to hear: that I simply conformed with the pack. People think, *Jocko is hardcore; he would* never *give in to the weakness of the pack.* But that would be wrong. If I were to hold my ground on this, if I were to "never give in," it would just mean that I thought my personal feelings were more important than the team. It would mean that my ego couldn't bear to step down and subordinate itself and conform to what the team was doing. It would announce to the world that I believed I was more important as an individual than the team. All of that is obviously the wrong attitude to have.

Let there be no doubt—the most important thing in a team *is the team.* Now, some people might think this is weak, but it isn't. The whole reason the team exists is to accomplish the mission. The more unified the team is, the more capable it is of accomplishing the mission. If I am causing a rift in the team, I am hurting our mission capability.

It goes further than that. Let's say some of the people in my platoon aren't in the best physical condition. If that is the case, obviously, I want them to be in better physical condition. To do that, they have to start working out harder. How can I get them to start working out? They don't work for me. I am the junior man in the platoon; I can't order them to do anything. I have to find another way. That other way is to *influence* them. To influence them, I have to build some kind of relationship with them. If I have no relationship, I have no influence. If I have no influence, I can't get them to do anything. I learned an important lesson: *I can't change the group if I am not in the group.* But if I am in the group, I can move it—maybe not as much or as quickly as I want to, but I can at least move it in the right direction.

To be in the group, don't be overaggressive. Don't alienate yourself from the group. Become part of it and earn your influence.

Does this mean you fall in line and conform no matter what to be part of the team? Absolutely not. You should maintain your individuality and unique personality and perspective. Just make sure your personality doesn't interfere with your ability to build relationships within the group.

But what if the group is bad? As I have said before, if it is doing things that are immoral, illegal, or unethical, you have to stand up; you have be smart about how you make your stand, but participation or passive approval of such behavior makes you culpable. I covered this in depth in the section about mutinies on page 56.

But what if the group isn't doing anything illegal or unethical but is doing things that are negatively impacting its ability to accomplish the mission? What if its members have a bad attitude toward leadership or toward the mission itself?

Once again, to dig in against them and form an antagonistic relationship with the team may not be the best way to help. If you alienate yourself from the group members, they will not listen to you, so try to bond with them. Build some relationships with members of the group so they actually listen to you. The stronger your relationships, the more people will listen to you.

You might have to make some compromises to build the relationships—not full compromises but enough to connect.

"This mission is stupid, and so is the boss!" someone might say to you.

If you reply, "No. This mission is awesome, and so is the boss!" that person is unlikely to listen to anything else you have to say. If they do listen, it will be only to catch some of the things you are saying and throw them back at you. This conversation will not end well.

Let's hear a different approach at the opposite end of the spectrum: "This mission is stupid, and so is the boss!" your coworker tells you.

You reply, "You're right, it is stupid. It is the stupidest mission I've ever been a part of. I can't believe the boss has us doing it!"

You've definitely showed your coworker you are in solidarity with them, but you have gone so far against the mission that it will be too hard to walk it back. You've also been disrespectful to your boss and to the company or unit. While disrespecting or disparaging the boss or the headquarters is a cheap and simple way to bond, it is also compromising to your character. So use extreme caution when talking about your leadership and the direction you are being given from them. This is not to say you have to fall on your sword to defend them, especially if they are doing things that are blatantly out of line. But even then, be tactful; don't be the person who is cutting down the chain of command or their vision when they aren't there to defend themselves. That is not a good way to go.

Try a more measured approach. You can subtly agree with your coworker's statement, but at the same time soften it and open a window for a conversation about it so you can start to move them in a better direction. When your coworker sounds off, "This mission is stupid, and so is the boss," instead of disagreeing outright on the one extreme or wholeheartedly echoing your coworker on the other, try an answer in the middle: "Well, it certainly is hard to understand the mission from our perspective. Why do you think the leadership has us working on it?"

Now, you and your coworker have something to discuss. And discussion, if it is civil, will grow the relationship. Furthermore, this statement asks a question. It asks your coworker to describe their perception of why the mission is being worked on. The answer will allow you to better understand their position so you can better counter them and get them on board.

As you build more relationships and have more balanced conversations with the members of the group, you will be able to exert more and more influence over them. This will give you the best possible ability to sway them in the right direction, not by fighting them head-on but by earning their trust and changing their minds indirectly from inside the group. This is the opposite of having an aggressive attitude and attacking the group's beliefs head-on. That will only leave you isolated from the group and unable to affect its direction in any way. Be balanced. Build relationships. Lead.

EVERYTHING IS GOOD
(BUT NOT THAT GOOD)

Bad things are going to happen. When they do, it is important for the leader to maintain a positive attitude, to find the good in the situation.

- *We were denied the funding we wanted? Good, we can learn to be more efficient.*
- *The mission we had been planning was canceled? Good, we have more time to prepare.*
- *The client we were about to sign walked away? Good, now we can focus on building better relationships with our other clients.*

No matter what goes wrong, there is always some good to find in the setback. A negative attitude will spread throughout the team, as will a positive one, so it is important for a leader to maintain a positive attitude.

But a leader can go too far with a positive attitude as well. If the team only hears positivity 100 percent of the time from the leader, the leader will come across as a Pollyanna who cannot see the reality of the situation. So a leader has to temper positivity with realism.

- *We were denied the funding we wanted? Okay, so this is going to take a little more time than we'd thought, but at least now we can streamline our processes and become as efficient as possible.*

- *The mission we had been planning was canceled? Well, that isn't ideal, but at least now we can rehearse some of the details and be even more prepared.*
- *The client we were about to sign walked away? This is not what we wanted, but it does give us the opportunity to focus on some of our other clients and build even stronger relationships with them, which will ultimately lead to more business.*

These more measured responses connect with the troops. If they think you are blind to the challenges presented by the situation, you lose credibility.

So while it is important to maintain a positive attitude about what is going on, don't ignore problems, and don't gloss over the trials you face. Be positive, but be realistic.

MANEUVERS

USING LEADERSHIP TO TEACH AND BUILD

When a person is placed into a leadership position, their perspective changes, and the new perspective often reveals to them the errors of their ways. Because of this, putting people into leadership roles is one of my most common remedies for a wide variety of leadership challenges. When it comes to teaching and mentoring people, there are many symptoms that cause me to give the same basic medicine. That medicine is to put the person in a leadership position. Leadership is a cure for an extensive assortment of problems.

FIXING A NEGATIVE ATTITUDE

When I was a young officer serving as an assistant commander in a SEAL platoon, I was friends with one of the assistant platoon commanders in another platoon. One day after work, he was complaining about one of the SEALs in his platoon. Actually, he wasn't really complaining about the SEAL, he was searching for a solution. It seems this particular SEAL had unlimited potential. He was extremely smart, charismatic, and athletic. He could have been a real asset. He had already done one deployment, so he wasn't a new guy anymore and was in a position where he could have some positive influence and impact on the platoon. Unfortunately, the influence he was having was a negative one. He was always looking to cut corners, complained about the training they were conducting, and consistently had a negative attitude about everything. Because he was smart, athletic, and charismatic, this negative attitude was starting to sway some of the other members of the platoon, and their attitudes started becoming slightly negative too. This was not a good situation.

I knew the young SEAL with the bad attitude, although not very well. I'd seen him around the team, and we'd been to some of the same SEAL Team gatherings. He wore his attitude on his face—too cool for school—as if everything were below him or didn't really matter. It was evident he was not an easy person to lead.

The assistant platoon commander wasn't sure what to do. He, the platoon commander, and the platoon chief had been trying for months to get the individual's attitude under control, but it wasn't happening. They had counseled him verbally, and the problem didn't change. They had assigned him weekend duty so he could "think" about his attitude, but that didn't help. They had even given him written counseling, which seemed to have made the problem even worse. The assistant platoon commander was at his wit's end on what to do. My suggestion surprised him.

"Put him in charge," I told him.

"What?" he responded.

"Put him in charge," I said slowly and clearly.

"Put him in charge?" the assistant platoon commander asked again, clearly caught completely off guard by my suggestion.

"Yes. Put him in charge. Let him shoulder some responsibility. You told me he's smart and charismatic. Sounds like there is some wasted talent there. He's probably not being challenged—he's bored. That might be the cause of his bad attitude. Don't let it be. Put him in charge of something. It will make him step up."

The assistant platoon commander didn't look very confident in what I was saying, but he was also out of ideas. "Okay," he said, "I'll give it a try."

He went on his way, and we carried on with our platoons. I went on a training trip with my platoon for a few weeks, and when we got back, the assistant platoon commander came looking for me and found me in my platoon hut working on some administrative duties.

"How's it going?" I asked, not really remembering the conversation we had had about his SEAL with the attitude.

"Not good."

I wondered what he was talking about. Then he continued, "He got worse."

I remembered the conversation we had had and was surprised. "Really?"

"Yes, really. I put him in charge, put some responsibility on him, and his attitude has become even more negative."

This definitely surprised me. I had seen this technique work many times in the past. When I was in the instructor cadre in the SEAL Team One training department as a young SEAL, when we had a SEAL going through training who had an attitude, often we would put him in charge of a training mission. The weight of that responsibility was almost always enough to straighten a guy out or at least pressure him to move in the right direction.

Responsibility had done the same thing to me. When I was in my first platoon, I was placed in the position of primary radioman. This was rare for an inexperienced new guy. There was a lot of responsibility for a radioman, not just with the preparation of radios but also in the planning for missions, which required detailed input from the radioman. It was a heavy burden for a new guy, and I felt the pressure. That pressure put my attitude on the right path; it made me work harder, prepare more, and take the job much more seriously than if I had been able to hide behind and rely upon a more senior radioman.

It became even clearer in my second platoon, when other young enlisted guys and I were trusted by our platoon commander to plan and run operations. All of us stepped up, had positive attitudes, and became better SEALs with that increased responsibility placed upon us.

I couldn't understand why this tactic had not worked on the individual in this other platoon.

"Really? That's bizarre," I said.

"Really. In fact, his attitude has gone backward. And it was almost instantaneous. As soon as I put him in charge, he got even worse."

Now this really puzzled me. How could it be that a young SEAL with intelligence, charisma, and athletic capability didn't want to lead? It made no sense. I couldn't understand it. Then a new thought occurred to me.

"Wait a second. What did you put him in charge of?" I asked.

"I put him in charge of cleaning the bathroom outside our platoon hut and emptying the trash every day. The tasks weren't even that hard!" he replied.

I shook my head. Obviously, I hadn't been clear enough.

"Noooo!" I said, distraught that this had happened and that I hadn't been clearer. "You needed to put him in charge of something that matters. Something that is important and that will challenge him. It's no wonder his attitude got worse! Putting him in charge of cleaning the bathroom? That's for new guys who screw up, not for a guy with a platoon under his belt who has a lot of potential! I meant you needed to put him in charge of running a training trip or leading a training operation."

The assistant platoon commander had a blank look in his eyes. He instantly knew that he had made a mistake. Of course the individual's attitude had gotten worse. For a guy with one platoon's worth of experience, cleaning bathrooms was not an opportunity to lead; it was a punishment. The assistant platoon commander shook his head.

"What do I do now?"

"Take him off bathroom detail! Tell him you realize he has way more potential than that. Tell him you want him to step up. Put him in charge of a mission."

"Well, we have some combat swimmer full-mission profiles to run this week. I can put him in charge of one of those."

"Perfect," I told him. Full-mission profiles were training missions where the platoon plans and then executes a training mission from beginning to end. *Combat swimmer* was the term we used in the SEAL Teams to describe our scuba operations, usually diving into a harbor, planting mines on a target ship, and then continuing the dive back to an extraction point. This would be a challenge for him, but I believed he could handle it. The assistant platoon commander agreed to give it a try.

I didn't have to wait long for feedback. A couple of days later, the SEAL with the bad attitude was put in charge of a full-mission profile training operation. I happened to see him walking around the team. He actually looked different. He was intent on what he was doing, looking purposeful and determined.

"How's it going?" I said to him as we passed each other in the hallway.

"Good to go," he replied.

The next day, the assistant platoon commander swung by my platoon office to debrief me.

"Unbelievable," he said as he walked through the door.

"What?"

"One-hundred-and-eighty-degree change in attitude," he replied.

"That's good to hear," I told him.

"But that's not all. He actually did a great job. An outstanding job. He oversaw the planning and execution of the entire operation. I thought he was going to need a lot of help, but he got it done. He asked a few questions of Chief and me, but it was all him. I'm impressed. And his attitude was the most impressive. And it's really sticking. He's not running the next operation, but he is still supporting the next guy. This worked perfectly, thank you," he said.

"No problem, brother. Glad it worked out. It's a good tool to have in your pocket."

With that, the assistant platoon commander walked out, and I solidified the idea in my mind that one of the best tools a leader has to help shape others is leadership itself; giving people responsibility and putting them in leadership positions teaches them to be better in a multitude of ways. And the more you understand that tool, the more accurately you can use leadership to teach people what they specifically need to learn.

TEACHING HUMILITY

We want our subordinate leaders to be confident, but confidence is a trait that can easily slide out of balance and inflate to the point where it becomes arrogance. A young leader, often fueled by success, allows their ego to get out of control, and they fall victim to a lack of humility; they believe their own hype, stop listening to other people, and stop planning and preparing like they should.

How do you teach some humility to a leader who has become arrogant? How do you put their ego in check?

Of course, life is the ultimate teacher of humility. If a person lives long enough and takes on true challenges, eventually they will get humbled. But that takes time, and as leaders we don't always have time for our subordinates to learn humility through the experiences of life itself.

So what did I do when I had to teach a young, overconfident leader some humility? I would put the young leader in charge of a mission or project I knew was outside their level of competency. "You've been doing such a great job, I want you to lead this mission. Okay?" I would say to them.

Usually, in their arrogance, they would be excited; they were thinking they were finally going to be in charge, which is exactly where they thought they belonged.

But the mission would be a difficult one—not an impossible one, not at all unrealistic—but hard enough that I knew they would likely fail.

Once they took charge and started to lead the planning process, one of two things would happen. The first possibility is that they would look at the mission, start the planning process, realize they were in over their heads, and come ask for help. But they could only do that if they were humbled. An arrogant person either doesn't want to ask for help, or thinks they can handle the situation, or both. But if they had an ounce of modesty in them, they would recognize their shortcomings, get a good dose of humility, and ask for help.

If they didn't ask for help, the second possibility would occur: failure. If the arrogant leader refuses to ask for help, they fall flat on their face, and they get humbled by the failure; they realize they aren't as awesome as they thought they were.

This does not mean I would let an arrogant junior leader fail on a real-world mission where lives were at stake, but training missions were a different story. Everyone who worked for me was put into leadership positions during training missions. Those who were cocky or arrogant were put into the toughest ones. They were humbled by those missions.

You can use the same technique in the business world. This doesn't mean you let an arrogant subordinate fail with a major client or lose the company a significant amount of money. Instead, you can either set up training projects for them or have them plan and lead projects for which there are minimal consequences. You can also stop them before they actually implement their plan and cause harm. There are even times when an arrogant young leader doesn't even know what it takes to put a plan together, so simply trying to come up with a cohesive plan is enough to humble them. Either way, there is no need to take unnecessary risk; the lessons can still be taught.

I am often asked, "But what if the arrogant leader does well? What should I do then?"

The answer is simple. First off, don't be disappointed; you have a leader on the team with a lot of potential. That is a good thing. But they still need to be humbled, so give them a mission that is more difficult. If they succeed with that mission, give them a more challenging one, then an even more challenging one. Keep cycling through that until the subordinate fails or asks for help. Once they are humbled, you can start to rebuild their confidence.

BUILDING OR REBUILDING CONFIDENCE

Just as there are times when subordinates are overconfident and need to be humbled, there are other times when we must build confidence in subordinates. Perhaps you have a subordinate who is new to their leadership position, and they don't feel comfortable leading yet. Or maybe they failed or performed poorly on a mission, project, or task and are now nervous about their ability.

The medicine for a lack of confidence is very similar to the medicine for overconfidence: put the individual in charge. Only now, when the individual needs confidence built, put them in charge of a mission you know they are capable of leading and executing well; you might even give them a mission that is fairly easy for them to accomplish.

The individual then steps up and does what they are supposed to do, and there is a positive result. Once that mission is complete, give them a slightly tougher one, and when that one is accomplished, a slightly tougher one to follow. With each accomplishment, their confidence will grow, and eventually they will be a confident leader. Then you can test their confidence with legitimately challenging missions.

Again, it is important to mitigate risk. Don't send a person who lacks confidence on a critical mission. They might not be ready and therefore fail, which will not only hurt the team but also bury the individual's confidence in a deeper hole. Use caution and select missions or projects that apply just enough pressure and carry low enough risk that they force the growth desired without overwhelming the individual or taking unnecessary risks to the overall strategic mission. At the same time, the mission can't be too easy or it will not put the individual under enough stress to actually build their confidence. They will think you tossed them a softball—which you did—and this will reinforce their own belief that they aren't good enough.

So find the balance and apply the right amount of pressure to encourage growth.

BUILDING HIGH-LEVEL TEAM PLAYERS

A person doesn't need to have a problem to benefit from being put in leadership positions. In fact, good leaders develop their teams by putting junior people in charge so they become more experienced and knowledgeable.

In my second SEAL platoon, our platoon commander constantly put us young SEALs in charge of training operations and evolutions. Once I had planned full missions a few times, it made my job as the radioman seem easy. I also had a better understanding of how my part of the planning fit into the overall mission.

This is a tradition I carried on when I became an officer. When I was an assistant platoon commander, our senior officer was grading my platoon on a series of operations. For the first operation, I put my most junior petty officer, Freddie, in charge of the mission. I helped him along the way, but he came up with the plan, prepared the briefing, and was placed in charge of executing the mission.

When we gathered for the mission briefing, the senior officer was there to grade and critique it. I stood up at the beginning and said, "Good afternoon, sir. We have been tasked with a mission that is going to be a pretty grueling gut-check. It is also complex with lots of moving pieces and involves some significant coordination. Our youngest and most junior petty officer will be the ground force commander for this operation. Freddie, it's all yours."

The look on the senior officer's face was priceless. It was obvious he had not expected me to put the youngest and most junior new guy in charge of the mission. I sat down next to him.

"Impressive," he said in a low voice. "Risky, but impressive."

"Negative, sir. Low risk. These guys know how to lead." I smiled back at him.

"Roger that, Jocko."

And they did know how to lead. Freddie did a great job on the briefing and a decent job on the training mission too.

Putting junior people in charge makes them better. It makes them understand what is going on way above their pay grades and how their jobs tie into the strategic mission. It is one of the best possible ways to develop subordinates to become not only better at their jobs but better leaders in the future.

Teaching humility, confidence, and creating high-level team players are only some of the areas where putting people in leadership positions is helpful. Leadership is a tool that can help you help your people. Use it.

LEADING PEERS

Leading peers is one of the most challenging types of leadership. When rank and position are equivalent, more tact is needed, and an even better relationship must be built. Once a relationship is built, you can use influence to lead the team in the right direction. This is not a bad thing, since influence is always the preferred method of leading. Influence is especially critical when leading peers.

Influence can be a challenge to develop with peers, because when rank is equivalent, egos often become even more visible. People are always looking to prop themselves up, to get an edge on others. If you allow your ego to manifest itself when working with peers, you will draw out the worst of your peers' egos as well. Egos must be subdued. Start with subduing your own. If you fail to subdue your ego, you will develop an antagonistic relationship with your peers. That will result in a *blue-on-blue,* the military parlance for *friendly fire,* which means you will end up destroying your own team. Don't allow that to happen. Take the high ground and put your ego in check.

One of the best ways to subdue your own ego and start building a relationship with your peers is by supporting their ideas. They might come up with a plan slightly different from yours, but if it is functional and will get the job done, support it. Let them take the lead. Don't feel the need to stick out your chest and flex your ideas; instead, support your peers' ideas. Even if you think your idea is better, if your peers' idea is close, go with it. The dedication they will have to successfully execute their plan will be far greater than the lackluster motivation they will have trying to execute yours. And more important, once you have accepted their plan, it shows them you are open to their ideas, and that means, in most cases, they will listen to your ideas as well. If their ideas have some shortfalls, explain the shortfalls and help your team members improve upon them. And don't look for credit once the idea is presented, even if you helped modify it into its winning solution; just give the credit to your peers. This is the beginning of a relationship and will increase your influence with them.

Next, when it is time to assign tasks, you should jump on the hard ones; shoulder the heavy weight for the team. If there is extra work to be done, take ownership of it and get it done. Of course, there is a dichotomy with this that must be balanced. If you are stepping up and taking responsibility for as much as possible, some peers may see this as a threat, as if you are trying to take control of everything, so don't go overboard. Monitor your peers' reactions, and make sure you are not being offensive by overvolunteering. If you sense they feel you are stepping on their toes, then back off.

Obviously, when things go wrong, take responsibility for problems and get them fixed. This is fundamental to the idea of Extreme Ownership, but of course there is also a dichotomy to be balanced. Just as taking on too many tasks can offend some people, there are also those who are offended if you try to resolve every problem. Always pay attention and be aware of other people's attitudes as you drive forward owning things and solving problems—you might offend some people.

If one of your peers' egos is out of control and they begin to maneuver to make themselves look good or even to make you look bad, don't fall into the ego trap. Don't attack them; simply continue to do great work and put the mission first. They might get some initial positive attention from their selfish actions, but eventually they will be uncovered. Take the high ground, or the high ground will take you.

As you put the team and the mission before yourself and keep your ego in check, you will begin to form relationships with your peers. This is the ultimate goal; if you have a relationship, you can then influence your peers. That is leadership.

Putting your ego in check can be very challenging. I like to play a game to put egos in perspective, and there are many ways to play it. I call it "Who would you hire?" or "Who would you promote?"

It works like this: Imagine you have two subordinate leaders working for you who are peers and are both running different, but similar, projects. They both fail to successfully complete their project on time. You bring the first leader in and ask him what went wrong.

"A bunch of things went wrong," he replies emphatically. "The material didn't show up on time. Our subcontractors were late on completing their part of the project. We had terrible weather that cost us quite a few days of work. And on top of all that, there were some conflicts between two of my shifts, and they weren't passing information to each other."

Clearly, this leader is not going to take ownership of anything. As a boss, you should not be happy at all with this attitude.

You call the next subordinate leader in and ask what went wrong with her project. Her attitude is different. "A bunch of things went wrong," she explains. "First of all, I didn't order the materials early enough, so some of them showed up late. From now on, I will be sure to order all materials earlier. I also didn't do a good job of keeping our subcontractors on track, and they were late completing their part of the project. Next time, I am going to do a daily check-in to confirm their progress and make sure things are on track. If they are not, I will make adjustments to get them on track and make sure they are not late. We also ran into some weather issues, and unfortunately I didn't have a contingency plan. On the next project, I will be informing everyone that days missed due to weather will be made up on the weekends so we don't fall behind. And lastly, two of my shift crews were not getting along very well, and I need to make sure they do. I will play a more proactive role next time to ensure all our teams are getting along well and are fully integrated, working together. Those are the things I am going to fix next time."

Clearly, this is a much different attitude, one of ownership and getting problems solved. Now ask yourself a question: Which of these two individuals would you promote to the next level of leadership? The answer is obvious. You promote the person who takes ownership and gets problems solved.

But even though that answer is so completely obvious, for some reason, when working with peers, people often fail to make that connection. They openly place the blame. They try to take credit when something goes well. And they think they are doing the right thing; they think no one notices that they are trying to make themselves look good next to their peer. But superiors and peers do notice, just as they notice when people are placing blame and not taking ownership, and they also notice people whose biggest concern is trying to make themselves look good. Don't do that. Put your ego in check. Support your peers and take ownership, and it will put you on the right path in the long game.

This is not to say that every boss will identify the self-serving subordinate immediately. Sometimes it takes time. Sometimes it takes a significant amount of time. Sometimes the self-serving peer will even get promoted because of the maneuvers they made. That can hurt, but deal with it. Don't get impatient. Play the long game. The truth will be revealed.

Do the right things for the right reasons. Support your peers. Stay humble. Take ownership of problems. Pass credit on to the rest of your team. Build relationships. That is how you lead your peers.

MICROMANAGING, INDECISIVE, OR WEAK BOSSES

Just as there are different types of people, there are different types of bosses. Some are far from perfect and leave much to be desired from a leadership perspective. Here are some common challenges you might face with your boss.

One familiar type is the micromanager. There are many reasons why people micromanage. The primary cause is a lack of trust; the micromanager does not trust their subordinates. So how do you deal with a micromanager? You have to build that trust. The way I built trust with micromanagers was by giving them all the information I possibly could and then performing well. To do that, I had to get over my own ego. From my perspective, I think I know what I am doing and that my boss has no right to tell me how I should do things or demand information about the minutiae I have going on in my world. But those thoughts are all from my ego. I have to reframe them in my head. Why does the boss want so much information? Because they care about the outcome of what I'm doing. Why do they want to tell me exactly how to do things? Because they have experience in the field and want to make sure I benefit from that knowledge.

Also, their impression of what is going on is often based on what

I am telling them, so if I am not giving them enough information to paint a clear picture of what is happening, it is my fault for not giving it to them, and I need to correct that. Finally, it is *my job* to build trust with my boss, not their job to give it to me; I need to earn it. If they want information, I am going to give them more than they could ask for. If they want to know what my plan is, I am going to give it to them in exacting detail so they have no questions left to ask.

When I do this over and over again, my boss will eventually realize that I am extremely thorough in my thought process. The boss will see that I think through the details like they do and will begin to give me leeway to execute on my own.

Then when I execute, I have to perform. That is the most important element in getting a micromanaging boss to give you some breathing room: performance. You have to execute well. Again, this might also require you to execute things *the way your boss wants to see them done.* That is fine. Do what your boss asks you to do. Flawlessly follow the minute directions the boss has given you. If something goes wrong, own it and brief your boss on how you are going to fix it. Then fix it and get it right the next time.

Then keep this up. A micromanager's attitude isn't going to change overnight; you have to show sustained performance to get them to back off. Don't get frustrated. Don't let your ego get the best of you. Push them information, and perform consistently. Build a relationship with them. Over time, they will give you trust and room to maneuver on your own.

What about when dealing with the opposite type of boss? The one who is indecisive about priorities? A common shortfall of an indecisive boss is hesitancy to Prioritize and Execute. They will say things like, "Everything is a priority," or, "We need to get everything done." The problem is if we spread our resources too thin over multiple priorities, we won't actually get anything done. We have to focus our efforts. But if the boss won't tell me what is most important, my team can't focus.

When I dealt with bosses like that, I used a fairly straightforward solution; I assessed and prioritized the list of things that needed to get done, and then I presented that list to my boss in a humble and tactful way so as to not offend his ego. I said something like, "Hey, boss, I know there is a lot to get done, and I'm going to get it all done. But to be efficient, I need to focus my resources a bit, so I wanted to run these priorities by you to make sure they make sense and reflect what your vision is so I can best support it. Can you tell me if you're good with the way I've prioritized them?"

Usually, that worked. Perhaps he made some minor—or even major—corrections to my list, but either way I now had a prioritized list to move forward with.

If that didn't work, and he still told me that "everything is a priority," then I tried to explain that I couldn't get everything done at once and that I needed to move through the tasks in some sort of order so I could properly focus my people and resources to get things done. That sometimes helped get him to give me priorities. If that still didn't work, I simply agreed with him and then came up with the priorities to the best of my ability on my own and moved forward according to them.

In creating my own priorities, I was not blowing off the boss or being disrespectful. Quite the opposite, in fact; if I want to get things done for my boss, I need to concentrate the efforts of my team. I can't do this if I don't know what is most important, so I will pick what I believe to be the most important thing and move forward on that. I am not ignoring other tasks or projects; I am simply focusing the efforts of my team so we can make progress and eventually execute on everything my boss has asked of me. Once again, I won't do it in an offensive manner; I won't throw it in my boss's face. I will quietly and subtly Prioritize and Execute.

I will also use tact when trying to get a decision out of an indecisive leader. Instead of saying, "Hey, boss, since you haven't made a call here, this is what I am going to do," I will say something more like, "Listen, boss, I know there is a lot going on, but I want to be proactive in supporting the vision you have, so in looking at which direction we should head, I'm thinking we should move forward in this direction here to most efficiently move toward your ultimate goal. Does that make sense? Because if we don't move forward, as you know, we won't meet the timeline for getting your project done."

I put the decision back on them, but I make it much easier for them to make it. Instead of having to sort through a bunch of complicated details, I have done all that for them. I am narrowing down their decision so all they have to say is, "Yes." I have also done it in a way in which my boss is clearly still the decision-maker; I am not stepping on their toes or offending their ego. My speech and my attitude are subordinate, which disarms them and allows them to give me the go-ahead on my plan—which, if presented correctly, should merely appear to them as an extension of their own. With these tactics, dealing with an indecisive boss can be handled effectively.

Then there are some bosses who are just plain lackluster. "My boss is weak; it is horrible!" I have heard this complaint over and over again.

I never looked at a weak boss as horrible; I always looked at a weak boss as an opportunity. If my boss doesn't want to come up with a plan, guess what? I will. If my boss doesn't want to clarify the mission, guess what? I will. If my boss doesn't want to take ownership, guess what? I will. And if my boss doesn't want to lead, guess what? *I will.*

But be cautious. As with micromanaging bosses or indecisive bosses, with a weak boss, you have to be careful when you step up to lead. Even the feeblest and weakest of bosses have egos, and if you offend them, they may lash out at you. So don't be offensive or overly assertive when you start to make things happen. Use soft language and frame things in ways that do not diminish the boss's ego but actually boosts it:

- *"Hey, boss, I know you have a lot going on, so I was thinking it might be helpful if I jumped on this project over here and moved forward with it. Would that be all right?"*
- *"Hey, boss, I'm sorry for being slow on the uptake, but I just want to make sure I fully understand your vision. Do I have it right when I say . . ."*
- *"Hey, boss, I'm trying to step up my game; would you mind if I took a crack at planning this next project so I can get some experience?"*

I will make sure I tell them what I'm doing and what decisions I am making in a humble, gentle way to make sure I don't step on their toes. If I step on their toes, it might be perceived as a power play or might offend their ego, and I don't want to do that. When I am tactful and keep my ego in check, I have no problem with a weak boss.

Some people might bemoan having a boss that is a micromanager, or indecisive, or who seems weak. I never worried about any of these. In fact, I'm fine with all of them.

If I am working for a micromanager, that means I am working for someone who is engaged and cares about doing a good job. Guess what? That's what I care about as well. If the person I am working for is indecisive, that's also fine with me. That means I can set priorities and guide decisions. And if my leader is weak, good, because if my boss isn't leading, then it means I can step up and lead.

Regardless of the shortfalls your boss has, it doesn't matter. Build a relationship with them. Do what makes sense to help the team accomplish the mission. If you do that, your team will win, and so will you.

WHEN TO MICROMANAGE

Some of the smoothest operations I led as a SEAL ground force commander—the overall person on the ground in charge of the mission—were operations in which the only direction I gave was the command, "Execute, execute, execute." Once I uttered those words, the SEALs in my platoon or task unit sprang into action. External security was set; compounds were entered; gates and doors were breached; buildings, hallways, and rooms were cleared; suspected insurgents were detained; searches were made—and all this happened with zero guidance from me.

Why? Because the guys knew what to do. They had a plan, followed the standard operating procedures, made adjustments where necessary to achieve the mission's goal, and got the job done. These situations are ideal. When the troops understand the mission, know the parameters they are allowed to work within, and have the skills to execute, then there isn't much left for the leader to do except sit back and await the outcome. Instead of looking down and in at what the team is doing, the leader can look up and out, observe what is going on outside the purview of the team, examine what awaits in the future, and plan the next moves the team is going to make. That is Decentralized Command at its best, the opposite of micromanagement.

But Decentralized Command and hands-off leadership don't always work. There are times when micromanagement is not only an option, it is a requirement. It becomes necessary when an individual or a group is not doing their job.

Of course, micromanagement is not the first option. Before taking that intense level of direct oversight, normal leadership procedures should take place. Make sure an individual understands the mission, the goal, and their specific role. Make sure they clearly understand the task required of them and all the expectations around that task. All of this can be done in a positive way that builds the relationship. If that doesn't work, a leader might have to get a little more specific while still being indirect. There is nothing offensive about saying, "Hey, I just want to confirm that I made it clear and that you understand exactly what your role is and how it fits into the strategic goal here."

But if an individual still fails to perform, the counseling will have to escalate; the leader will eventually have to be very direct. "Look, this is exactly what you need to do, and here is how you have to do it."

In addition to verbal counseling, at this point, you as the leader might have to micromanage the individual or the team. You might need to show exactly what needs to be done, perhaps even do it so they see with their own eyes exactly what is expected of them. Then monitor them closely; watch them do what they are supposed to do. Follow up with them. Check in with them. Micromanage them. Depending on how they react, you might actually need to explain to them what you are doing and that you are well aware of the fact that you are micromanaging them, telling them something like, "Listen, I know it may seem like I am breathing down your neck and micromanaging you, but I just want to make sure you know exactly how to execute. Once you have got this under control, I will give you the space and freedom you need to operate without so much oversight from me."

Then, once they start to get on track and begin successfully doing what they are supposed to do, you can back off a little bit. As they show continued success, you can back off even more. However, if they fall off track, you simply tighten up the micromanagement again. Then once they are back on track, give them more room. Eventually, once they are executing properly, you can back off and let them run on their own.

Of course, there is a chance that even under close micromanagement, an individual or a team does not improve over time. Obviously, micromanagement is not a permanent solution; leaders cannot place all their focus on one individual or one team for an extended period; there are other people, other teams, and other issues that need their attention as well. When leaders have to focus heavily, micromanaging one person or one team over a long time, other things start to slide. That is not acceptable. If that happens—if an individual or a team cannot do their job efficiently—and leaders are investing too much time in that one individual or that one team, then the leader has to give clear notice of the expectations and the consequences of not meeting those expectations: "If you don't get up to speed on this—if you don't execute this job how it is supposed to be executed—you will not have this job anymore. You will be terminated." In the case of an underperforming team, leaders have to address the leader of that team: "If your team doesn't get up to speed and perform to expectations, I am going to remove you as the leader." Once these clear expectations are delineated, if they are not met, then the next step is obvious: terminate the individual or remove the leader from the team.

Micromanagement is a tool, but it is not a permanent solution. Use it, but know when it has reached its limitations, and then remove or replace personnel to fix the problem.

THE BOSS WANTS ALL THE CREDIT

If your boss wants all the credit, the answer is simple: give it to them. It is that straightforward. The only thing that makes this challenging is your own ego. That is because you don't want them to get the credit. In your mind, you are the one who has done a bulk of the work. You are the one who put in all the long hours. In your mind—and maybe in reality—you have done everything. So why should the boss get the credit?

This answer is also simple: because they are the boss. That is why. And as the leader, they are going to get credit whether you like it or not. What are you going to do? Raise your hand and say, "Actually, it is *I* who deserves all the credit"? No. That doesn't work. Asking for credit is a horrible move to make in any scenario. And in a scenario where your boss is asking for credit, it is an even worse move, because if your boss is asking for credit, it means they are likely insecure. They want that credit to build up their ego, so if you try to take it away from them, it is an attack on their ego, and they will not be happy. They will not trust you, and you will form an antagonistic relationship with them.

Don't do that. Instead, let them have the credit. Don't be jealous and bitter. Accept the idea that as the boss, whatever they did—or didn't do—allowed the team to accomplish the mission. Maybe they just got out of everyone's way. Maybe they were micromanaging like crazy. It doesn't matter, because whatever they did, if the mission was successful, then it worked. So let them have the credit.

This can really bother some people. They will ask, "What if the person isn't a particularly good leader and the only reason projects are being completed is because of individual contributors on the team?" My answer is, this is why we have to play the long game. Unless the leader is completely and utterly inept, which could require a mutiny (see the section "When Is Mutiny in Order?" on page 56), then the devil you know is better than the devil you don't know. A marginal leader with whom you have a good relationship can be a benefit to you and the team as long as you have built trust with its members. Based on that relationship, the job gets done and the team—and the boss—gets credit.

Some people worry that if a low-performance leader gets credit, they might get promoted, regardless of the skills they lack. And that is true; if a boss leads successful projects or missions repeatedly, they probably *will* get promoted.

But remember, when they do get promoted, they will need someone to take their place. Chances are, they will select someone they trust to fill their vacancy. Someone who has supported them. Someone who was humble enough to let them get the credit they wanted for the team's effort. If you have played the game correctly, that person will be you. Remember, this promotion isn't for your own self gain but for the team; once you take the boss's position, you can lead the team and execute the mission in the best way possible. Since you have trust established, you will continue to lead your team and influence your boss so they make good decisions for the good of the team.

Some people also fear that if they give their boss all the credit, then they themselves will never get the credit they so badly deserve. To overcome this fear, first, obviously, put your ego in check. The main reason you want that credit is to satisfy your ego. Once you have done that, relax. If you are working hard and making things happen, credit will eventually come your way. Be patient. And when credit you have not asked for comes your way, it is doubly valued, since you simultaneously appear highly competent *and* humble, which is a winning combination.

So if your boss wants the credit, put your ego in check and give it to them. Your humility and leadership will be rewarded in the long run.

THE NEARLY INDEFENSIBLE LEADER

It is always good to support your leader. If you undermine a leader, it not only hurts them, it also hurts the morale of the troops as well as you as a subordinate leader. You are setting an example; if the example you set is one of disrespect up the chain of command, you can expect much the same from the people you are leading.

When presenting a plan to your troops that you don't necessarily agree with, you could say, "Well, I don't agree with this plan, but it is what the boss is telling us to do, so we have to do it anyway." Clearly, that is not a good approach. They will see you don't believe in the plan, and if you don't believe in it, why should anyone on your team believe in it? And if no one believes in it, then why on earth should the team actually execute it?

When a decision is made or a course of action comes down from the chain of command, you must execute it as if it were your own. Sure, you can debate your boss behind closed doors about what course of action you think is best, but once the decision is made, you get on board and execute to the best of your ability. You tell the troops, "The boss and I talked through this for quite a while. And when you look at it from all the different angles, especially considering some of the bigger-picture effects, I think this is the best solution for how we execute. Let's get it done."

The way you present plans to your troops is similar to the attitude with which you treat your boss. Your boss may not make all the best decisions. He might be awkward or say the wrong things at the wrong times. Maybe the troops have a go at him and throw some verbal jabs in his direction behind his back. Do not join in that. In fact, stop it. This doesn't mean you throw yourself on your sword and blindly defend him, but instead you explain that "the boss has a lot on his mind" or "the boss's job is to run the company, not keep us entertained." These types of statements let your team know that while the boss isn't perfect, he still needs to be respected for the job he does.

But there are times when the boss can be nearly indefensible. Perhaps she is egotistical or arrogant. Maybe he is condescending to the troops. Or maybe the boss makes bad decisions over and over again.

In these cases, blindly defending the boss will put you at odds with the team members; they see and know the boss is horrible, and if you blindly defend them, your credibility takes a hit. But that doesn't mean that openly belittling or disparaging them is a good option. That behavior from you leads to complete disrespect from the team and a failure of good order and discipline. You have to balance defending the boss with connecting with the troops. Here are some phrases that convey the right message—that even if you don't have the highest regard for your boss, you still value the importance of accomplishing the mission.

- *"Listen, the boss might not be perfect, but he is driving us toward the same strategic goals we want to accomplish."*
- *"Look, the boss might not be ideal, but she still gives us the support we need. The better we perform, the more support we will get."*
- *"The boss has some quirks, but we know where he stands, so we work with him to the best of our abilities, which means dealing with those quirks so we can get the job done."*
- *"Complaining about the boss doesn't get us anywhere, and it doesn't make our jobs easier. What we can do is try to form a good relationship with her so we can influence her in the right direction."*

These statements balance the delicate dichotomy between simply backing the boss with unconstrained commitment and showing some level of hesitation. And that is exactly what a leader has to do when their boss is nearly indefensible.

Of course, there are times when a leader becomes truly impossible to defend. The cases are rare, but when a leader is doing things that are illegal, immoral, or unethical or is making such bad decisions that the mission or the troops are at real risk, then it is time for the subordinate leader and the subordinates themselves to consider going above the boss in the chain of command—or even, in the absolute rarest of cases, to consider a mutiny (see page 56).

STRESS RELIEF

Almost every job creates some level of stress. Salespeople deal with angry clients. Police face criminals day in and day out. Construction workers face the physical hazards of their jobs and the complexities inherent in their projects. Teachers deal with unruly students. Software engineers have deadlines to meet. Food service workers contend with hostile customers flying off the handle because their steak was overcooked. Stress exists at some level in every job. When people succumb to stress, it can be extremely bad for the individual, the team, and the mission. How does a leader prevent an individual from being overstressed?

The first thing a leader needs to do is something they should already be doing: build a relationship with his or her subordinates. Why is this such a common theme in my leadership principles? Because having good relationships up and down the chain of command is one of the most important leadership elements for any successful team. And one of the reasons it is important is that it will help the leader manage the stress of his or her subordinates.

As a leader, if you have a good relationship with your subordinates, you will talk to them, they will talk to you, and you will *listen*. There is a decent chance they will let you know if they are feeling an inordinate amount of stress. This is an obvious and straightforward way of knowing that someone on your team is feeling undue pressure.

But there is also a chance they may not tell you they are feeling stressed. Perhaps they are embarrassed. Perhaps they think it will put a promotion at risk. Perhaps they feel stress but don't recognize the symptoms because they have never experienced it before. These are only some of the reasons your subordinates won't tell you they are stressed.

This is another reason why relationships are so important. If you have a relationship with your people, you know them; if you know them, then you know when they are not acting like themselves. Perhaps they are less talkative. Maybe they are becoming easily aggravated about little things. Maybe they are looking disheveled. Whatever the change is, it is a change, and a change in behavior can be a sign of stress.

Major Dick Winters, commander of 2nd Battalion, 506th Parachute Infantry Regiment, made famous by the HBO miniseries *Band of Brothers*, which is about their exploits in the European campaign in World War II, pointed out a sign that indicated a man was reaching his breaking point. In his book *Beyond Band of Brothers,* he wrote that he knew someone was going to crack when he saw him with his helmet off and his head buried in his hands. At first, I didn't quite understand how he could have been so sure, but then I thought about what that looks like visually, and I realized he was completely right. When you see a person with their head sunken down, hanging into their hands, it is obvious they have had enough.

So what do you do with a person who is struggling with stress? Give them a break. Give them a rest. Take them out of the stress-inducing environment. When Major Winters would see someone approaching their breaking point, he would assign them temporary duty away from the front lines. He wouldn't tell them he was doing it because he thought they needed rest; that might have triggered shame and made them not want to go. Instead, Major Winters would figure out some kind of task that needed to be done in the rear and then send the individual in question on the "mission."

I did the same thing as a platoon commander and as a task unit commander. If I saw stress start to negatively impact one of my men, I would assign him a logistics run to headquarters for a few days or send him to liaise with a unit in a relatively nice area where he could get some rest. Like Major Winters, I wouldn't tell my men I thought they needed a break; I would tell them I had an important task that needed to get done and I trusted them to make it happen. They would get a few days of operational downtime and come back recharged.

The best way to treat combat stress—and any stress—is to remove the affected individual from the stress-inducing environment. After some rest, the person will usually return to their normal behavior. I liken the human mind under stress to a car when the Check Engine light suddenly comes on. Sure, the engine can keep going for a little while, but what the engine really needs is service. If the engine gets serviced, it will be fine and return to normal, but if the engine is not serviced and the driver continues to push it, eventually the engine will burn out and fail catastrophically. It will be completely destroyed.

The same thing can happen to the human mind if kept under stress without relief. For a clear image of this, watch any film of shell-shocked soldiers from World War I. They were pushed to the limit without relief, and they broke mentally. They were no longer able to function at all.

Don't allow that to happen to your people. Know them. Watch them. And when they need a break, give it to them.

PUNISHMENT

Punishment must be dealt out at times, but a good leader should need to use it seldomly. If a leader gives good, clear guidance about what needs to be done, how it needs to be done, why it needs to be done, and what the consequences are if it is not done correctly, the troops should carry out what has been asked of them.

If for some reason your troops don't execute the plan, then, of course, you should first look in the mirror. Do not assume the troops have simply decided not to do what was required of them; instead, assume you did not give them appropriate direction and that is the reason for the transgression.

If you have confirmed that a rule was violated or direction not followed even though it was understood, some punishment must be meted out. Again, this should be rare, because if a leader is doing his or her job correctly, members of the team will understand what, how, and why they are doing what they are doing and execute appropriately. The need to punish someone on the team is almost always a direct reflection of the leader and the failure to lead appropriately. This might seem extreme—and in fact it is. It is Extreme Ownership.

- *If a team member is late, perhaps the leader failed to explain the importance of being on time.*
- *If a team member fails to complete their portion of a project, perhaps the leader didn't give the support required.*
- *If a team member drinks alcohol and gets into trouble with the police, perhaps the leader failed to set clear parameters around drinking.*

This list could go on indefinitely. A leader is always responsible for the actions of his or her subordinates. This could be extended even further by saying that if there is a team member who is a troublemaker, the leader should preempt trouble by removing that individual from the team.

Even with complete Extreme Ownership in place, which will

eliminate most failures to follow rules within a team, there are times where team members are negligent, malicious, or willfully disobedient. When this happens and when lines are crossed, punishment is necessary. One key component of that statement is *when lines are crossed*. That means there has to actually be lines that are clearly defined and rules that are clearly understood. To punish an individual for the infraction of an unwritten rule is usually inappropriate, unless the behavior is grievous enough that any reasonable person would deem it out of line. Barring that level of violation, unless rules are clear and documented, it is difficult to punish an individual for their judgment, however far off it might be. This is not to say you as leader cannot counsel for bad behavior; obviously, you should. But actually punishing someone for a violation that isn't clearly defined isn't good practice.

It is also good policy to lay out the consequences for violations. No one should be surprised when they receive a punishment, and knowing what they are risking in terms of punishment will eliminate much of the need for it.

Once the rule and punishment for violation have been clearly established, if the rule is broken, handling it is easy: administer the punishment. Sure, there can be some level of circumstantial consideration, and mercy should not be seen as weakness. A leader who considers mitigating factors will be seen not as lenient but as sensible. To show clemency is not being a pushover; it is being understanding. Those are not bad things.

My SEALs sometimes broke the rules. Perhaps one got into a

fight while out in town. Maybe another didn't submit the required paperwork for a training event. Whatever the infractions, I would weigh them against the individual's historical performance. If he had a great record and the violation was uncharacteristic of his normal behavior, I would give him some slack. If the individual was a habitual rule breaker, he would receive the full punishment. If a violation has been committed and there is no legitimate reason for it or any mitigating circumstances, then simply hold the line and dispense the punishment as defined.

Administering punishment is one of the less appealing parts of leadership, but it is sometimes necessary. The better you lead, the less you will need punitive action, but you will sometimes still need it. Deliver it with justice.

WHEN TO QUIT

One of the mantras in the SEAL Teams is "Never quit." That is one of the main refrains utilized during basic SEAL training, and it makes a lot of sense during that training because that is how you make it through: you don't quit. No matter what training evolution comes along, no matter how hard it is, no matter how tired, sore, frustrated, exhausted, or otherwise broken you are, *you don't quit.*

That is how you make it through the training, and that is how you eventually become a SEAL. But when you get to the actual SEAL

Teams, that extreme attitude has to be adjusted. It has to be modulated, because if it isn't, it can lead to disaster.

The classic example of this is the young SEAL leader who has made it through basic SEAL training and shows up at a SEAL Team. He has heard the mantra "Never quit" thousands and thousands of times. He has yelled it to his friends and whispered it to himself. It has become ingrained in his head.

Now he is at a SEAL Team, and he is tasked with developing a plan for a training mission. He does his best, but because he is inexperienced, the plan is marginal. After briefing his squad on the plan, they head out to execute the mission. It soon becomes evident that the plan is ineffective. Maybe he picked a bad route or the wrong approach to the target, or maybe he underestimated enemy resistance. Maybe the weather was inclement and threw off their timeline. He could have misjudged any one of the countless variables that impact a mission, but whatever the variable, it has rendered the plan ineffective.

But the young leader has been trained not to quit. He won't give up. He presses forward, expending all his resources, energy, and time to stay the course. Still the squad fails the mission. But beyond failing the mission, they are completely spent or compromised and unable to do anything else; they can't even support another mission.

That is wrong. He should have quit, returned to base, reformulated his plan, rested his troops, and reloaded to take another shot at executing the mission.

I used to run a training problem to drive this point home to young SEAL leaders. The scenario would be in an urban environment in a fairly large building with a long hallway with multiple rooms along it and one large room at the end of the hallway at the opposite end from where the SEAL platoon would enter. In the room at the end of the hallway, I would emplace what we called a *barricaded shooter*, who would have a massive, powerful paintball gun capable of shooting devastating fire and with a virtually unlimited supply of ammunition.

The barricaded shooter would also be bunkered in, meaning that he would be in a miniature pillbox built of sandbags and plywood that almost completely encased him, save for the barrel of his paintball gun, which would be sticking out of a small hole and pointed down the hallway.

The SEAL platoon would be tasked with clearing the building, and inevitably the leader would quickly come up with a fairly simple but generally straightforward and effective plan following the standard methodology: sending two SEALs into the hallway to clear the first room, after which they would send two more for the next room, then two more for the next room, and so on, until they had all the rooms in the hallway cleared, which meant the entire building was cleared.

But with this barricaded shooter in position, when the first two SEALs entered the hallway, they would be gunned down. The training cadre would be there to enforce the situation and would tell the first two SEALs they were "dead," at which point, they would lie down.

The young SEAL leader, now hearing the commotion and the shots fired, wants to know what is going on, so he peeks through the doorway that enters the hallway. He sees the first two SEALs sprawled out on the ground, not moving, clearly "dead."

So what call does he make?

"Give me two more! Go clear that first room!"

At this point, the next two SEALs in the assault force, anxious to get after it, step past the young SEAL leader and into the hallway. They barely get past the other two "dead" SEALs, when they, too, are gunned down with a murderous spray of paintball. The training cadre declares them "dead" as well, and they lie down on the floor.

The leader once again hears this unfolding and peeks around the corner to assess. Now he sees four of his SEALs piled up in the hallway covered in paintball. What does he decide to do? "Two more! Go!"

Hearing this, the next two SEALs barrel past the leader, through the door, and into the hallway, where they, too, are slaughtered by paintball.

Now it is obvious there is a big problem. Clearly, there is a devastating threat. What to do? The young SEAL leader thinks he knows.

"Give me two more! Now!"

Two more SEALs enter the hallway of death and soon meet theirs as paintballs riddle their bodies. This time, though, the leader exposes himself a little; he watches them enter the hallway and sees them get gunned down from the room at the other end. He sees the silhouette of a barricaded shooter. He now clearly understands the situation. So what does he do?

"Barricaded shooter, end of the hallway," he announces, letting everyone know what is going on before giving his next order. "Two more! *Go!*"

With that, two more SEALs enter the hallway and are promptly massacred by the barricaded shooter. Then the leader calls for two more, and two more after that, and he continues to send men until no one is left except the young SEAL leader himself. He thinks he knows what he must do, so he takes a breath, charges down the hallway, and, like the rest of his men, is hit head to toe with paintballs and "dies" in a blaze of glory.

He was the last man. Now, everyone in his platoon is dead. The team has failed.

But at least the young SEAL leader didn't quit, right?

Wrong!

There is a time to quit. In this training situation, once the scenario was over, I would discuss it with the young SEAL officer. We would examine the result, which was clear: the objective was not achieved and everyone was dead. Obviously, this outcome is horrible, and he would never want it again. I would then explain to him the difference between the strategic objective and the tactical one— and that it was okay to quit a tactical plan if it wasn't working, especially if not quitting a tactical plan or objective was actually going to hurt our ability to reach a strategic objective. In this case, how much good was his platoon to the strategic mission now that everyone was dead? The answer is clear: zero.

The next iteration of training, I would put him in a similar situation, sometimes even the exact same scenario in the exact same building. The same thing would happen: the first two guys would enter the hallway and be killed. The same thing would happen to the next two. If the young leader wanted to stay the course again, I would intervene.

"What are you doing?"

"Taking the hallway."

"You're doing the exact same thing you did last time."

"But we need to clear this building, and that means getting down this hallway."

"What did we just talk about?" I would ask, surprised the connection hadn't been made. I would then see a flicker of thought in his eyes.

"You mean . . . I should quit?" the young officer would say cautiously.

"You should quit *this plan*. It isn't going to work. You have already lost four guys. I know this is just training and they will be miraculously resurrected after this iteration, but if this were real, that's four of your guys dead. Gone. You need to rethink this."

"But I can't just run away. We have a mission."

"Okay. Take a step back. Detach. Look around. Do you think maybe there is another option?"

"This hallway has to be cleared. It leads to every room in the building."

"The building has to be cleared. And the hallway does lead to every room. But are there any other access points to the rooms, especially to that room at the end of the hallway with the barricaded shooter?"

The young officer would sit puzzled for a few seconds. Then I would look at one of the windows and give a quick nod.

"Windows. That room has windows. We can go in through there."

"Good thinking," I would reply with a smile. With that, the young officer would give a quick tasking to one or two fire teams to move externally around the building and clear the room with the barricaded shooter through the windows.

The troops would quickly go into action, throw some grenade simulators into the target room, which would wound or at least startle the barricaded shooter. Then the troops would enter the room through the windows and eliminate him. The platoon would learn a new approach to solving a problem, which is actually an old approach—it is called a *flanking maneuver*. And, more important, the young officer would learn that it is okay to quit.

And I get it; perhaps *quitting* is the wrong word. It really should be called a *retreat*. We aren't giving up completely. We aren't surrendering. We are simply giving up on one approach that isn't working to try another.

That is another important way to frame this—by looking at it from a tactical versus a strategic perspective. In military parlance, *tactical* means the immediate situation right in front of you, the actual existing battle that is happening here and now. *Strategic* is the broad, long-term, overall objective you are trying to achieve. For example, a tactical objective might be trying to take a hill or a section of a city, whereas a strategic objective might be removal of a tyrannical leader who threatens the stability of the region he is in, which creates a clear and present danger.

It is okay to quit on a tactical objective; maybe you don't take that hill or clear that sector of the city right now. Perhaps the enemy was too strong and heavily defending the hill and the city. To secure the objectives would be too costly in men and matériel, so instead you have to bypass those objectives or put them off until a later date— you have to quit the tactical objective.

But you don't quit the strategic mission. If you have made the strategic assessment and decision that this tyrannical leader must be removed for the safety and security of your nation, then you have to drive on; you cannot quit your strategic aims.

There are even times when quitting a tactical mission might be a necessity for the success of the strategic mission. General George Washington led the retreat of continental forces out of New York, an escape that was crucial for the ability of the revolutionary army to continue to fight later engagements.

A similar situation happened during World War I after a long campaign in the peninsula of Gallipoli with extensive casualties to the British, Australian, New Zealand, and French forces; the Allies made the decision to abandon the campaign—to quit. But this allowed those troops that were evacuated to be used in other theaters of the conflict, which contributed to the eventual strategic victory for the Allies.

And, of course, almost everyone knows of the retreat across the

English Channel from Dunkirk. Over three hundred thousand Allied troops were evacuated so they could live to fight another day. They quit the tactical battle and were able to fight on and defeat the Axis powers.

These are some of the many examples of situations where a leader must decide to quit, to retreat, to abandon a plan and accept a tactical defeat, in order to regroup and come back to fight at a later time for a strategic victory.

Sometimes you have to quit on a short-term tactical goal—you have to retreat. But never quit the strategic mission. Never give up on your long-term strategic goals.

COMMUNICATION

KEEP THE TROOPS INFORMED

The primary mode of transportation for SEALs is the foot patrol. Sure, airplanes, helicopters, and boats are how we travel long distances, but, nine times out of ten, the way we make our final approach to a target is the same way soldiers have moved into battle for thousands of years: on our feet.

The distance traveled varies depending on the operation. It can be simply the last hundred yards after being dropped off by a helicopter right next to a target, or a patrol can cover scores of kilometers over many days and nights of movement.

When the military is portrayed in movies or on television, foot patrolling usually appears to be a simple, relatively benign action much like a walk through the park.

But foot patrolling is no walk through the park. It is a physically hard, mentally challenging, sometimes painful evolution that can be the most difficult part of an operation. Every member of the patrol is weighed down with weapons, ammunition, helmet and body armor, radios, batteries, grenades, medical gear, food and water, and other special equipment for specific operations. At a minimum, every member of the patrol is carrying 50–70 pounds of gear, and at a maximum, the weight carried can approach 120 pounds. Combine that weight with steep and unforgiving terrain, the necessity often to move at night with low visibility over long distances, and the stress of needing to stay alert for enemy movement, and patrols can quickly go from simple walks to excruciatingly painful endeavors that sap operators of their energy and morale.

As a young SEAL, I went through a block of training called SEAL Tactical Training, or STT, with the rest of the new guys who reported to SEAL Team One with me. It was the first thing we did when we got to a SEAL Team. The training was supposed to build on the absolute basics we'd learned during BUD/S and prepare us to be assigned to a SEAL platoon. In addition to expanding on the basics, the instructor cadre had us learn the fundamentals and then perform the roles of the various jobs in a SEAL platoon to give us an understanding of the positions we might fill.

That meant I did patrols as a heavy machine gunner, medic, point man, rear security, or even as the patrol leader. Each one of those jobs placed me in a different position in the order of march of a squad when going on patrol. I was lucky enough to have walked in all the various positions on many patrols before I was assigned a permanent role in my first SEAL platoon as a radioman.

In a SEAL squad on a foot patrol, the point man is up front, leading the way, followed by the patrol leader. After the patrol leader is the radioman, then the first machine gunner, then the medic, then another machine gunner, followed by the assistant patrol leader and, finally, rear security. When a SEAL platoon, which consists of two SEAL squads, is patrolling together, the squads patrol in sequence, with squad one leading the way and squad two bringing up the rear.

So each SEAL's position in a patrol is dictated by their job inside the platoon or squad. Having the opportunity to walk in all those positions taught me a very valuable lesson about leadership.

As point man, patrols were physically harder because you were breaking trail, but there was a benefit: you knew what was happening. As point man, you actually steered the patrol; you were up front, constantly looking at your map, checking off terrain features that you had studied, counting your paces so you knew how much distance you had traveled, and regularly assessing exactly where you were and how much farther you had to go.

The next man in the line of march was the patrol leader. As patrol leader, you also had a good understanding of where you were. In that position, you worked closely with the point man, who had done a map study with you and who would point out prominent landmarks that indicated where you were and how much farther you had to go. Whenever the patrol took a break to rest, which was supposed to happen for ten minutes out of every hour, the point man and patrol leader would study their maps together, shoot bearings with their compasses, and triangulate the exact position of the patrol.

The radioman was the next in line, located in proximity to the patrol leader so he could provide communication to and from the patrol leader to external supporting assets like aircraft and artillery. Accordingly, the radioman was also well informed; he watched the point man and patrol leader's map study, and he listened as they discussed how much farther it was to the target, what terrain the patrol was approaching, and when the patrol would be stopping again. Furthermore, when the patrol leader needed to pass information up the chain of command—like the position of the patrol or the distance to the target—it always went through the radioman, so he was always aware of what was happening.

After the radioman was the first machine gunner, and he was often the first level of disconnect in the patrol. Out of earshot of the patrol leader, the machine gunner wouldn't be able to hear any discussions between the point man and the patrol leader. The medic was next in line, now five people back from the front of the patrol. He was barely able to keep a grip on what was happening and where.

The medic was followed by the second machine gunner. Often, the second machine gunner was so disconnected he would just blindly follow the man ahead of him. He was followed by another man, and then another, and then another, each separated farther and farther from the point man and the patrol leader, each with less and less information.

Eventually, you got to the men in the tail end of the patrol, who had hardly any information. The less information you had in a patrol, the more miserable it was. You wouldn't understand where you were, how much more distance had to be traveled to get to the target, when the next break for rest would come, what terrain features were around. You had no idea if there was a giant hill to climb up or a river to cross. All you could do was put one foot in front of the other and suffer. Morale would diminish, and you could feel the patrol ready to fall apart completely.

But the suffering and the lack of morale wasn't the worst part. The worst part was your tactical situation. You had no idea where you were. If the enemy attacked, you wouldn't know where to go. If you got split up from the rest of the platoon, you would be lost. Knowing where you are is the most important piece of information on the battlefield, but you didn't have that.

Because I had walked all the different positions, I realized that the farther back in the patrol you were, the less you knew. Every time I served as the point man, patrol leader, or radioman, I understood everything so much more clearly because I was aware of what was happening. When I was on the tail end of a patrol, it was like being in the field with a bag over my head. I hated that feeling.

So whenever I served as the patrol leader, both during training operations as a young enlisted SEAL and then when I eventually became an officer where I served as squad leader, platoon commander, and task unit commander, I made it my mission to ensure that everyone in the patrol knew exactly what was happening. In the mission briefing, I reinforced the importance of passing signals as we patrolled. I ensured that everyone knew and understood the route we would be taking, with a serious focus on significant terrain features that I knew everyone would be able to easily identify. Then, once on patrol, at each rest stop, I would bring my map around to each man or each team leader and explain where we were, how much farther it was to the target, and what terrain features to expect. I would check on their condition too: how much water they had left, how their feet were doing, how tired they were.

But it was not only the comfort and welfare of the men I was looking out for. Lack of knowledge on the battlefield is tactically unsound for a squad, platoon, or unit of any size. Troops that know what is happening remain engaged, prepared, and operationally capable of doing their jobs with efficiency and high morale. Uninformed troops are a disaster waiting to happen.

This obviously does not only apply to tactical patrols. In any leadership situation, it is critical for the leader to keep everyone on the team as informed as possible. When the team members don't know where they are, where they are going, or how much longer they have to go to reach an objective, they are lost. When people are lost, they don't know in which direction to move. They don't understand how their efforts impact the strategic mission. They can no longer effectively do their jobs. Morale plummets.

The hardest part of this from a leader's perspective is understanding that the team doesn't always see what you see. Team members aren't given the information that you have, and assuming they do have that information is careless. You have to be proactive in updating your troops. You have to continually keep them abreast of what is happening. And you can't count on them to ask questions either; they might not know what they don't know. Don't assume they know anything;

in fact, assume the opposite—that they know nothing—and then take responsibility as the leader to keep the troops informed at all times.

RUMOR CONTROL

If rumors are running rampant in your organization, you have created the environment to allow them to grow. The environment that rumors grow in is one in which there is a lack of information. If you don't tell people what is going on, they will make up their own versions, and their versions will not be pretty ones.

So get the word out ahead of the rumors. Just like on a patrol, you need to keep the troops informed. Need to lay some people off? Explain why. Have to discontinue a product? Tell the troops why. Shutting down an office? Communicate the reason to your people.

All these subjects are tough to cover. It is easy to find excuses not to talk about them, and it is certainly more comfortable to keep your mouth shut and hope no one notices. But they absolutely will notice, and they will fill in the reasons with their own ideas. Need to lay some people off? The rumor will be, "We are going out of business!" Have to discontinue a product? Same thing: "We are going out of business!" Shutting down an office? Now it is certain: "*We are going out of business!*"

Don't allow this. Get aggressive and attack rumors by getting ahead of the bad news and telling your team what is going on. Be truthful, be direct, and be timely. The longer you wait, the larger the rumors grow, and the harder it is to get back under control. The quicker you share the truth of what is going on, the better it will be received and the fewer problems you will have with rumors.

CLEAR GUIDANCE

If your subordinate leaders or frontline troops aren't doing what you want them to do, the first person you should check is yourself. The most likely cause of this problem is unclear or misaligned guidance.

Make your guidance to the troops simple, clear, and concise. More guidance does not necessarily make guidance clearer; in fact, more guidance can actually make things more confusing and convoluted. It is also important to ensure that the guidance given at every level of leadership is aligned. While there might be differences in the details at different levels of an organization, the guidance that underlies the message must be the same.

When I was a commander of Task Unit Bruiser deployed to Ramadi, Iraq, the rules of engagement, which were supposed to explain to the troops how and when they should engage the enemy with lethal force, were very complex and difficult to understand. The document was several pages long and filled with verbose legalese. The message was muddled by phrases like "enemy military and paramilitary forces" and "reasonable certainty that the proposed target is a legitimate military target." While these phrases might be simple to understand for a mature person sitting in a comfortable place, a young, frontline SEAL operator might have trouble remembering what a document said when they read it and parsing out the meaning under the stress of combat conditions and while needing to make a decision that will determine the life or death of another human being.

Because of this, I translated the rules of engagement for my team into simple language that could be more easily understood: "If you have to pull the trigger, make sure the person you are killing is bad." This is as simple as I could make the rules of engagement, and it made sense. When observing people with unknown motives and intentions, it was always difficult to ascertain if they were hostile or not. Those people often acted in suspicious ways and did things that were unexpected. But there was a clear line of hostility when they started to do something offensive toward coalition forces. Once that line is crossed and hostile offensive action is taken by an individual, it is clear that person is bad and needs to be engaged. This is an easy decision for a frontline shooter to make.

It was also important that my team understood *why* it was so important to follow the rules of engagement. So I explained to them, again very clearly, that if one of them were to kill or injure an innocent civilian, it would have a major negative impact on all our efforts in the campaign. I explained that we were there to protect the civilian populace, so any harm done to them was completely contrary to our mission and was absolutely unacceptable.

This guidance was clearly understood by everyone in my task unit, which is the way guidance should be, but it can be hard to ensure everyone actually comprehends. The best way to ensure that people understand isn't by simply asking them if they understand. Too often, that will just result in people nodding yes because they don't want to admit their lack of comprehension. The best way is to ask them to explain the guidance back to you in their own way. Perhaps even quiz some members of the team on some scenarios that require them to understand the guidance. If they can do this, then they understand.

It is also important to communicate guidance through as many channels as possible. Send it in written form. Speak to the troops face-to-face. Record a video they can watch repeatedly. Repeat the message over conference calls. Have your subordinate leadership do the same things. Different people absorb information in different ways. Make sure your guidance is propagated in as many ways as possible so it will impact the variety of people you have on the team in a way they best understand so it can be absorbed by all of them.

BECAUSE I SAID SO

"Because I said so!" parents sometimes shout at their children. Clean your room because I said so. Be home by ten o'clock because I said so. Do the dishes because I said so. Wear a helmet while you are skateboarding because I said so.

If you are a parent who uses such language, you might eventually use it with your employees or subordinates if you aren't careful. And you will be wrong. In fact, you are even wrong to use this language with your children.

Let's take the skateboard example. I live by the beach in Southern California, where skateboarding is enormously popular. The tricks and stunts are almost unbelievable to watch and can be dangerous, with the biggest danger being smacking your head on the pavement. So wearing a helmet is a good idea.

If you were to tell a child, "Wear a helmet because I said so," what are the chances of this being effective? Sure, if you are standing there watching her, imposing the rule on her, she will wear the helmet. But what about when she is a couple of years older and she is skateboarding on her own with her friends? What are the chances that she will listen to you then? It won't take long for her realize that helmets are uncomfortable, they are hot, they are somewhat cumbersome, and, most important, they aren't "cool." So as soon as the child is out of your sight, she removes her helmet. "Because I said so" doesn't carry any weight when I am not around.

But what if, instead of just telling your daughter, "Because I said so," you explained why you wanted her to wear a helmet? If you explained to her the dangers of falling off her skateboard and hitting her head? And then what if you actually took her to a hospital and showed her another kid who had fallen off his skateboard, hit his head, and was now lying in bed with severe brain damage, unable to walk, talk, or feed himself? What if you took your daughter to a graveyard and showed her the grave of a ten- or eleven-year-old boy who had died from falling off a skateboard and hitting his head? Would that leave an impression? Absolutely. Your daughter would be much more likely to wear a helmet and even tell her friends to wear helmets. The difference is actually explaining the *why—why* it is important for her to do what you are asking her to do.

"Because I said so" is clearly not the best way to get someone to do what you want them to do, and it is not a good way to lead. That might seem obvious, but "Because I said so" gets used in many forms: "It's my call," or "This is my project," or "I outrank you." All of these are just another form of "Because I said so," and they all are about the equivalent in terms of their leadership effectiveness—that is to say, not very effective at all. None of those statements will get your subordinates to put forth their best effort to accomplish the mission. They will simply be carrying out orders and will not execute with any real enthusiasm or tenacity because they don't really understand why they are doing what they are doing.

Don't lead like that. Instead, explain to your subordinates *why* they are doing something. Explain why it is done a certain way. Give them the reason why a task, maneuver, or procedure is important and how it not only affects the team, the company, and the mission but also how it affects them.

There is another important reason not to say, "Because I said so," and that is because you might be wrong. If one of your subordinates asks why you are asking them to do something a certain way, and the only reason you can give is "Because I said so," this is an indicator that *you* don't know the reason why. And if you don't know why you are doing something, then *why are you doing it?*

I was working with a tech hardware company that was trying to get their first major project launched. Like many young companies, they were understaffed and undermanned, but they had a job to do. I was explaining to a large group of engineers and the executive team, including the CEO, how important it was to understand *why* you are doing what you are doing. I told the frontline engineers that if they didn't understand why they were doing what they were doing, they needed to ask their supervisor.

One of the engineers asked, "What if my supervisor doesn't know?"

I replied, "Then ask your supervisor's supervisor."

"And what if they don't know?" the engineer shot back.

"Then ask the next one up, and then the next one, and then the next one." Then I looked at the CEO and said, "As the CEO of this company trying to deliver this piece of equipment to market, do you want anyone in this organization working on something if not one single person on the team can explain why it is important?"

"Absolutely not," the CEO responded, "absolutely not. With the amount of work needed to make this launch happen, we need every single person working on critical tasks. If no one in your chain of command can explain why something is important to the execution of this mission, then I don't want you doing it."

So explaining *why* not only ensures the frontline troops can execute with understanding, it is also a way of ensuring the frontline troops aren't wasting time and resources on things that don't matter. And "Because I said so" defeats all that benefit. So if you find yourself saying, "Because I said so," stop, assess, and give your subordinates, *and yourself,* a real reason *why.*

THE THREAD OF WHY

I had just addressed the majority of the workforce from a large corporation I was working with. I introduced the Laws of Combat and the principles of Extreme Ownership. When I was done, the CEO of the company got up and made a speech explaining that the company had turned around and actually made money for the first time in two years—a good amount of money too—and that this profit had made the shareholders very happy. He was clearly excited about this. But he didn't quite get the reaction he'd expected from the crowd. They sat and listened quietly with no cheers or applause to meet his passion—just awkward silence, not at all a reflection of his enthusiasm. By the time he was done, there was an obvious gap between his attitude and the crowd's.

He walked offstage confused by the reaction of his company. I could see by the look on his face he was surprised that this group of employees and leaders weren't excited about this incredible turnaround that the company had undergone and by the profits that had been delivered to the shareholders. The CEO, the COO, and I walked back to the CEO's office to debrief.

"That didn't go the way I'd expected it to," the CEO said.

"Me neither," added the COO.

"My fault," I said. "I should have reviewed your speech and thought a little more about it."

"What was wrong with my speech?" asked the CEO. "It was nothing but good news. We have cut expenses. Gotten rid of unneeded personnel. And I even explained *the why* like you recommended—the fact that we are doing all this to become profitable! And we were successful in doing just that, becoming profitable for the first time in two years! What's not to like?"

The CEO was right. From his perspective, this was all good news. The problem was that he didn't understand how his words sounded from the perspective of the troops, and I had failed to listen and assess that beforehand. So I told him.

"The problem isn't that it wasn't good news. It's that from their perspective, it looks different. I have been working with your frontline leaders and managers for the last couple of months, and they see and hear things differently. When you say, 'We have cut costs,' they hear, 'You got rid of some of the supplies and resources we relied on to do our jobs.' When you say, 'We got rid of unneeded personnel,' they hear, 'You fired my friends and now we are even more undermanned than we have ever been.' Even when they hear your reason *why*, 'We are profitable for the first time in two years,' they hear, 'Some stockholder somewhere is making money off the hard work and sacrifice we are making to get the job done.' Their perspective is very different from yours, so it needs to be framed in a way that makes sense to them."

I could see the CEO recognized the truth in what I was saying. "But the message is what it is. The facts are the facts, and it is a positive message. How can I frame it any better? The company makes money, and that money goes back to the shareholders. That's the way it works."

"Like I said," I told him, "you need to frame it from their perspective; there has to be a thread that connects the *why* back to them. That thread looks something like this: We were profitable for the first time in two years. What this means is we can put more money back into advertising. The more advertising we do, the more leads we get. The more leads we get, the more customers we get. More customers means more sales, more sales means a lower cost to produce our product. The lower the cost to produce, the lower and more competitive price point we can offer. The lower the price point, the more we sell, which once again will lower our cost to produce, which will make us even more money we can put back into advertising to generate even more sales. And what this cycle means to everyone in this room is growth of the company, and growth of the company means not only long-term job security but also opportunity—for increased responsibility, for increased leadership, and to make more money. That is *why* profitability is important to everyone in this room. When this company succeeds, every member on this team succeeds as well, professionally and financially. So thank you all for your hard work and dedication. When the individual wins, the team wins. And when the team wins, the individual wins as well."

It didn't take any further explanation. The CEO got it. "All right, I need to send out an email to the troops explaining the *why* better. Maybe even a video. I missed the mark, but I can fix it."

"You can, indeed," I told him, and we got to work putting together a communication to the entire company further explaining the *why*.

This is a lesson learned for any leader. Explaining the *why* is important. But the *why* has to tie back and connect to everyone in the chain of command. Success for "corporate" or "profit for the shareholders" is not great motivation for everyone. You have to think about how the mission and outcomes benefit the whole team and then explain that. The frontline personnel likely don't care about how much money the shareholders are going to put in their pockets, but they will care if that profit helps their job security and opportunities for professional growth.

It is the same for military operations. You have to explain why a mission is important not just strategically for the country but how that impacts the frontline troops: "This mission will disrupt the enemy's mortars attacks on our base," or "This mission will put a dent in the enemy's ability to gather intelligence and stage assaults on us," or one from the bigger picture, something like, "If we can stop the enemy here on their turf, they won't ever get the chance to attack our turf, which means our families will be safe."

No matter what the mission or the goal, the troops need to understand how it will positively impact *them*. So make sure the thread of *why* explains that to them in no uncertain terms.

TACTFULLY DELIVERING THE TRUTH

When delivering criticism, it is important to do it with consideration and delicacy. If you punch someone in the face with criticism, they will become defensive and are unlikely to take the criticism on board, so a more indirect approach is needed.

First: care about your people. If you truly care about them, they will know that, and they will accept your criticism more easily. Next: take ownership of the problem. Of course, Extreme Ownership should be the fundamental principle utilized by any leader, and there are tactics of employing Extreme Ownership when trying to critique a subordinate. Utilizing Extreme Ownership while providing feedback might sound like this:

- *Instead of saying, "You failed to get the project done on time," use, "What support or assets could I have given you so that we could have gotten the project done on time?"*
- *Instead of saying, "You failed to meet the mission objective," try using, "I don't think I did a good job of explaining the mission objective. Did you fully understand it?"*
- *Instead of saying, "Your lack of professionalism caused this client to go to our competitor," try saying, "I think I have allowed things to get too slack around here in terms of our professionalism, and I think that's one of the reasons we lost that last client to one of our competitors."*

It is important to note that these are not simply techniques you are utilizing so your pesky subordinate falls into line. That is not the point. The point of all these statements—and the whole point of taking ownership—is that you must truly believe what you are saying. And you should, because the ownership statements in those examples are not simply lip service. They are true.

- *If a leader follows up with the team members and makes sure they have all the support and assets needed to complete the job on time, then it will be done on time.*
- *If a leader correctly explains the mission in a simple, clear, concise manner and then ensures it is understood by the team, then the team will accomplish the mission.*
- *If a leader fails to emphasize the importance of professionalism, then it should come as no surprise that subordinates fail to act professionally.*

I'm often asked if there are any scenarios when the leader is not fully responsible for the performance of his or her team. The answer is *no*. If a team is not performing, then it is the leader's fault; the leader has not trained and mentored the team members to where they can accomplish the mission. If a team doesn't have time to train, then the leader has not made training a priority or run it up the chain of command to get the support needed. If members of the team are simply incapable of performing the duties required of them, then the leader hasn't done his or her job of removing the substandard performers.

Ownership is real, and when utilized correctly, the concept of ownership will spread. So when a leader says, "What support or assets could I have given you so that we could have gotten the project done on time?" usually a subordinate will say something like, "Well, boss, I could have used another person on one section of the project. But the reality is, if I would have done a better job planning and utilized my man-hours more efficiently, we would have finished on time. It won't happen again, boss."

Just like that, the problem is solved.

But, of course, there are situations when the subordinate in question does not respond to indirect criticism. In those cases, it is necessary to escalate the directness of the critique. It is still not a license to be overly harsh; leaders should maintain tact even when providing more direct critique. Here are some examples of slightly more direct approaches that still don't attack the individual:

- *Instead of saying, "What support or assets could I have given you so that we could have gotten the project done on time?" a more direct critique would be, "This is your project, and you are the one I trust to drive it to an on-time completion. What else do you need to ensure that happens?"*
- *Instead of saying, "I don't think I did a good job of explaining the mission objective. Did you fully understand it?" a more direct critique might sound like, "You were the leader of this mission, and we didn't achieve the objective. Did you not understand what the objective was and the importance of it? If not, what can I do to ensure 100 percent that next time you do understand it?"*
- *Instead of saying, "I think I have allowed things to get to slack around here in terms of our professionalism, and I think*

that's one of the reasons we lost that last client to one of our competitors," an escalation in this critique might be more along the lines of, "I think I've allowed things to get too slack around here. As a leader, you need to hold the line as well. A lack of professionalism just won't cut it in this business."

That more direct approach may very well solve the problem, but if it doesn't, and further escalation is necessary, a leader might have to explain that if the situation is not rectified, the subordinate will be written up. If that doesn't work, then the leader will have to follow through and give a written counseling to the subordinate, documenting for the subordinate exactly what the problem is, what the expectations are, what corrective measures need to be taken, and the consequences of failing to meet the expectations.

Once this full escalation of counseling has taken place, there is not much left for a leader to do. If the individual continues to fail to meet standards, it is the leader's duty to remove the individual from that position and either put them in a position they are capable of or remove them completely from the team.

BALANCING PRAISE

When I was commander of Task Unit Bruiser, we were doing our predeployment workup training cycle, which consisted of different tactical training blocks preparing us for a combat deployment. One of the most dynamic and intense blocks of training is called *close-quarters combat,* or CQC. This training consists of moving through buildings tactically, clearing them of enemy personnel, marshalling innocent people, recovering any hostages, and safely departing the building. We train with live-fire ammunition, live explosive breaches, and even live sniper shots. Altogether, it makes for some high-stress training that demands top performance from every member of the team.

We had a solid task unit. Our leadership was smart and engaged. Our midlevel SEALs were freshly returned from combat deployments. Our new guys were humble and eager. We put in extra time and effort to be ready. Before the training even started, we were reviewing and rehearsing the standard operating procedures we would use to clear buildings. We followed the four Laws of Combat. We always utilized Cover and Move, we kept our plans and our communications Simple, we identified our biggest problems and Prioritized and Executed on them, and we operated with fully Decentralized Command, which allowed every member of the team to act based on their understanding of the mission statement and the commander's intent and to make decisions that supported the mission.

The principles worked well. During run after run through the kill house which is a vast building with ballistic walls that SEALs and other special operations groups utilize to rehearse CQC—we did well. Of course, many individual mistakes were made, and we didn't always perform perfectly as a team. But when we did make mistakes, either from a personal or a leadership perspective, we always owned them, figured out solutions, and implemented them as quickly as possible.

When an individual had a problem, the whole team rallied around that individual, invested extra time, and got them up to speed.

As we approached the end of our second week, the instructor cadre threw a massively complex problem at us. Multiple buildings, multiple simultaneous breaches, dynamic movement—it was chaos. But the task unit grabbed ahold of the chaos and got control of it. Problems were solved. Targets were hit. And the problem was solved quickly, carefully, and efficiently. We were doing well.

But then disaster struck. Not in the form of enemy personnel or an even more complex problem but a disaster of our collective egos.

After we finished the complex problem, we gathered around the instructor cadre for the debrief. They mentioned a few minor mistakes, but then the senior instructor, an experienced and respected master chief, stood up and blurted out, "This is the best task unit we have ever had come through here! You guys are absolutely crushing this!"

A couple of hoots let loose from the task unit; there was an audible joy in hearing those words. But they made me instantly shudder. I was worried that egos would soar and guys would lose focus. "I wish you hadn't said that," I said as I walked by the master chief. "They are going to let down their guard."

He shook his head and replied, "They'll be fine."

I wish he had been right, but he wasn't.

The next run through the kill house was an unmitigated disaster. Guys missed targets. They didn't clear corners or follow other simple standard operating procedures. The head counts were off. Assaulters got bogged down in hallways and rooms. The clearance took an eternity. It was a failure—the complete opposite of the iteration we had just completed, which was all but flawless. Now we were a mess.

Once again, we surrounded the cadre for a debrief. The instructors hammered us about a litany of mistakes and errors, both on the individual level and on the leadership level. But none of them hit on the real problem, so I chimed in at the end of the brief.

"You want to know what happened?" I asked the task unit. No one responded. "I'll tell you. You got complacent. The master chief gave us all an incredible compliment after that last run, and that was really nice of him, and sometimes it's nice to get some positive feedback, but there was a major problem—you all took it to heart. You believed it and lost focus. All of you. Me too. We lost our humility. We all let down our guards, and we fell apart. Now, let's go back in there and annihilate this target. With aggression. With precision. And with vengeance. *No slack at all.* Zero. Any questions?" No one said a word. "All right, then, let's lock and load and go do this the way it's supposed to be done."

And that is exactly what we did. We got back on track and performed at the level we were capable of.

The lesson had been learned—or should I say *relearned*—as I had seen this happen time and time again during my service in the SEAL Teams. You have to use caution when you dole out praise. Too much praise and people, consciously or unconsciously, back off their efforts just a little bit. Multiply that times a whole team of people and you get a negative impact.

Of course, there is a dichotomy; praise should be given when warranted. But it must be given judiciously, and it should be tempered with a goal that requires the team to still push. Instead of "This is the best task unit we have ever had come through here!" try "This is the best task unit we have ever had come through here, and if you push harder, you will set a new standard. Let's see if you can shave another two minutes off your clearance time." That way, the team members have something to strive for. They will want to go even harder.

At the same time, it is also important to not become the leader who is never satisfied. If you move the goalposts farther down the field every time the team does something well, that can dampen morale as well; the team members will eventually become jaded and stop putting forth the full effort since they know they will never actually win.

One thing I always did to mitigate excessive praise was to direct praise at individuals instead of at the team. Instead of saying, "Team, you did an amazing job on that operation," I would call out specific people. "Mike, nice job getting that room with all the obstacles in it cleared. And Jim, outstanding work marshalling the civilians; you handled that perfectly. And the three of you locking down the back side of that target did an awesome job."

Individual praise would let everyone know that I was impressed when things went well, but it was not a blanket statement that everyone would get to enjoy. To be recognized by me, you had to bring your A game. When I retired, I heard stories from guys about how they were always looking for my praise—doing their best in the hope that I would give them a compliment of some kind. When I did, they would feel like they had earned it. Then they would go out and try to earn it again and again, continually trying to do their best work. And it showed, because when you multiply that attitude across a whole team, the results speak for themselves.

So remember—praise is a tool, but it is a tool that must be wielded with caution. Too much and it can cause people to let up and rest on their laurels. Too little and the team can lose hope. Which also means that if your team members are losing hope and their morale is fading, some well-placed compliments can go a long way. And if you see troops getting overconfident, a few critical remarks can put them in check. Either way, remember that when you are a leader, your words will impact the behavior of your subordinates and the team more than you might think. Think before you speak, and measure your words carefully.

HOPE

"We hope the weather holds."

"Hopefully, the enemy doesn't have any sentries in that position."

"We are hoping the competitors don't try to grab any market share in that area."

Statements like these are obviously not good. As we said in the military: hope is not a course of action. You cannot rely on hope. You have to plan. You have to consider contingencies. You have to stack the deck in your favor. You cannot have hope play a role in planning or execution.

But hope does play a role in leading and in winning. While hope must not be a course of action or a pillar of planning, it must be present in the hearts and minds of the people executing the mission. If there is no hope for relief or success or victory, the will cannot endure. Without hope, there will be surrender.

This is why you are responsible for sustaining and maintaining hope within the team. Explain to the team that victory is possible. Explain how it will be achieved. If victory is too far in the distance, designate some shorter-term victories that can be achieved so the team knows it can win and, through that knowledge, maintain hope.

In cases where victory is impossible but retreat is not an option, explain how driving on even in the face of imminent defeat is a victory in its own right. Holding the line and giving everything will at least build your reputation as a team. And with that reputation, each and every member can go on to their next chapter with their heads held high, ready for their next challenge. And that attitude is hope enough to fight on.

ULTIMATUMS

Ultimatums are not optimal leadership tools. Like digging in, they allow no room to maneuver. No one likes being trapped and controlled. But there are extremely rare times when ultimatums can and should be utilized: when enough is truly enough. Then an ultimatum can be used, and when it is used, the leader must hold the line and adhere to it. Never make an ultimatum you can't keep.

MAKING AN ULTIMATUM AS THE BOSS

If you feel you have to issue an ultimatum to your subordinates, one of the first things you should ask yourself is, *Where did my leadership fail?* Because the fact of the matter is, as a leader you should be able to get what you need out of your subordinates through solid leadership, not ultimatums. Explaining why a task is important to the strategic mission and how achieving that mission will ultimately benefit everyone on the team should be enough to get people to do what they need to do. That is no easy feat, and sometimes it takes considerable time and effort to communicate that information properly.

But sometimes, no matter how hard you try, you can't get the message through. In those cases, ultimatums are a tool of last resort after all other efforts to get an individual to do what they are supposed to do have failed.

Once an ultimatum has been delivered, it cannot be reversed, which is one of the biggest problems with giving them. Ultimatums, by their very nature, are immovable and cannot be adjusted. This makes the people you delivered them to feel trapped, and no one likes feeling trapped. If you do make an ultimatum and do not keep it, your credibility will take a hit.

All that being said, if you have done everything in your power, if you have coached, mentored, and persuaded an individual to do something and they still will not do it, then it might make sense to give them an ultimatum. Make it explicit, not only in the requirements of what needs to be done but also in the consequences of exactly what will happen if the ultimatum is not met. Use no uncertain terms, and ensure that the individual fully understands.

While utilizing ultimatums for an individual can make sense in some rare cases, they should be used even more rarely on teams. If you put an ultimatum on a team for something it must do cooperatively, some members might change their attitudes and performance while others might not. If that happens, you will be stuck trying to decipher who tried to make adjustments and who didn't, which will be challenging. Instead, if it is absolutely necessary to impose an ultimatum on a collective effort, place it squarely on the leader. Then that leader can work with the team to deliver—or not—and bear out the repercussions. If the team gets the job done, the leader will know who on the team got on board and who didn't and can deal with the team members accordingly. If the team fails to get the job done and deliver on the ultimatum, you as the boss know exactly who to deal with: the leader of the team.

MAKING AN ULTIMATUM AS A SUBORDINATE

An ultimatum is a threat and a power play, so making one up the chain of command is a high-risk move. An obvious example of this is when a subordinate says, "If I don't get a promotion, I'm leaving the company." Most bosses are not going to like that *at all*. Instead of putting an ultimatum on your boss, perhaps you should try to figure out why you aren't getting promoted in the first place. Maybe you aren't doing the job as well as you think you are. Maybe other candidates for promotion are performing better. Maybe someone else is senior to you. Maybe the company isn't promoting anyone. Maybe you just don't deserve to get promoted yet. Whatever the case may be, there is very little chance that making a demand for a promotion is going to work—and even if it does and you get promoted, there will be damage done. You have revealed the limits of your loyalty to the team, and you have placed the importance of your own promotion above the importance of the team and the mission. That will be remembered.

This same underlying negative essence will be in just about any ultimatum that is made up the chain of command. Instead of making an ultimatum, have legitimate discussions with your boss and explain your position and your thoughts. But don't make ultimatums up the chain of command.

Now, if there is some rare situation in which you have completely exhausted every possible option to inform your boss of an outcome and it is not getting through, *and* you are actually going to go through with an alternative solution, then it makes sense to let your boss know. But I would think of it as a warning, not an ultimatum. If you have been fighting for a promotion and done all the right things, asked all the right questions, been in position long enough, and are factually the best candidate, then it might be okay to let your boss know, "Boss, I have been here for six years; I really love being here and want to continue to work here. But I also have a family to support and provide for, and I need to do what is right for them. I know there are other opportunities in other companies for me to advance. Even though I don't want to, if I can't get some upward mobility here, I might have to start looking at some alternative companies where I can further my career."

That is about as gentle as you can make it. But many bosses will *still* be offended by it. That is why you shouldn't do this unless you have to. And you should not do it unless you mean it; make sure you know without a shred of doubt that there are other opportunities out there that you can move toward.

Of course, demanding a promotion isn't the only time a subordinate might consider making an ultimatum up the chain of command. Maybe it is a request for more support. Maybe it is a request for a pay raise. Perhaps it is a demand for a piece of equipment or additional funding. Regardless of what the ultimatum is, the reception from up the chain of command will almost always carry the same sting, so use *extreme caution* when delivering one.

DEALING WITH AN ULTIMATUM PLACED ON YOU

While no one likes ultimatums and they are not good leadership tools, unfortunately leaders do sometimes impose them on their subordinates. Usually they are a last resort, used in situations where all other instruments of leadership have failed, which usually means the demands being made are impossible—or close to impossible—to meet.

So what should you do when your boss puts an ultimatum on you? Tell the truth.

You should start with telling yourself the truth. Do a hard, honest assessment of the situation and figure out if what you are being tasked with is actually possible. Are you making every possible effort to achieve the task? Is there anything else you and your team can do to get the job done? If the answer to these questions indicates that you can do more, then redouble your efforts and *do more.*

You should also tell your team members the truth. Let them know that the ultimatum has been placed on you and thereby the team, and explain why you are all going to dig in and do your absolute best to get the job done.

Hopefully, after pulling out all the stops and getting after it like you have not before, you and the team are able to deliver on the ultimatum. You get a high five from your boss, tell your team well done, and move on to the next task or project.

Unfortunately, that doesn't always happen. Often, the reason ultimatums are given is because the task or project was an extremely difficult one, perhaps even impossible. Even after you and your team go into hyperproductive mode and put forth maximal effort to get the job done, sometimes it just isn't enough. So what should you do then?

Again, the answer is to tell the truth—only this time, to your boss. First, figure out if there are any other measures that might help you accomplish what you have been asked to do. Perhaps you need more people. Maybe you need more funding. Perhaps you need to let some other tasks slide while you focus on getting the ultimatum fulfilled. Once you have all the information you need to explain the situation to your boss, explain that, despite the ultimatum, you will not be able to accomplish what he or she has asked you to do. Describe what you would need to get the job done and what will happen if you do not get what you need.

If you have done a good job of communicating with your boss and they have enough humility to listen, after you detail the situation, they should recognize the truth and withdraw, or at least modify, their ultimatum. But that is no guarantee. Bosses who resort to delivering ultimatums might not be rational enough to listen to reason and could hold the line on it. If that happens and your leader maintains the course, then simply knuckle down, do your best, protect your team to the best of your ability, and stand by to suffer the consequences with your head held high. Don't be spiteful. Don't have a bad attitude. Don't disparage the leader. And don't give up. Maintaining your dignity and the morale of the troops is the victory in a case like this.

REFLECT AND DIMINISH

A leader must have control over his or her emotions. Letting emotions drive decisions is a mistake. This does not mean leaders are devoid of emotions, but it does mean they have to learn to direct and modulate them. There are times when emotions must be shown to make a point or to connect with others.

Let's say one of your subordinates comes into your office, face red with anger, and shouts, "*This is ridiculous! The supply department didn't deliver our materials on time! That's two weeks in a row now, and we will probably miss our deadline!*"

Clearly, your subordinate needs to calm down. But don't tell them that; if you tell your subordinate, "Listen, buddy, you just need to calm down," your words will have the opposite effect—your subordinate will get even angrier. They will be frustrated that you don't understand what is upsetting them, and it will convince them that you have zero clue about the *cataclysmic effect* the failure of the supply department will have on the entire organization! By telling your subordinate to calm down, you have also just opened up a chasm between you two. You are on one side, and your subordinate is on the other. Instead of opening their mind, your subordinate now shuts down and doesn't hear anything else you have to say, and no progress will be made.

So instead of starting an adversarial conversation with your subordinate, become an ally. A good way to go about doing this is the Reflect and Diminish technique. *Reflect and Diminish* means to reflect the emotions you are seeing from your subordinate but diminish them to a more controlled level. So when you subordinate comes in fuming and screaming about the failure of the supply department to deliver materials on time, instead of telling them to calm down, raise your voice a little bit to reflect the anger, but diminish that emotion a little bit so it isn't as strong as theirs and starts to de-escalate the situation. It might end up sounding something like, "You've got to be kidding! How late are they with the delivery?"

With that statement, and the emotions reflected, you are now on your subordinate's side. "Two days!" your subordinate replies, still mad, but with less venom.

Now you can settle down a little bit more too. "Two days is way too long. We need to fix that permanently. But we also need to do something to fix the predicament that you're in. How can I help you make that happen?"

Within this brief exchange, the situation has settled down, and you and your subordinate can start to solve the actual problem at hand.

This works with just about any emotion. If someone is sad, reflect but try to diminish that sadness a little bit. If someone is envious, mirror a little of that envy so you can then explain what envy really is (their ego!), and they will actually listen to you. Even when someone thinks a comment or a situation is funny and you don't, telling them to tighten it up and be serious is going to make them think you don't have a sense of humor (and a good sense of humor is critical for leaders). So instead, smile, maybe chuckle a little bit, and then explain why you *both* need to take things a little more seriously. Because your subordinate sees you have a sense of humor, and because you connect with them, they are much more likely to listen to you.

This technique works up the chain of command as well as down. Don't isolate yourself emotionally from your team members. Instead, foster shared emotions—reflect their emotions but diminish them so they de-escalate, and you can focus on actually solving the problem at hand. Reflect and Diminish.

WHEN TO YELL AT SUBORDINATES

When is it a good time to yell at your subordinates? Almost never. Of course there are situations when you have to yell—like when there is a lot of noise or you need to get the attention of a larger group. Such situations are about volume, not emotion; in these cases, you have to yell simply so people can hear you. But there is a big difference between yelling because you need to deliver your message with more volume and yelling with emotion. Yelling because you are angry, frustrated, panicking, or otherwise emotional is weak leadership, and your team members will mimic your behavior. If you get angry, so will they. If you get frustrated, so will they. If you start to panic, so will they.

If you are yelling because they don't understand what you are trying to say, you are wrong. Yelling at them makes them feel *they* are doing something wrong; but the reality is that if your people do not understand your explanation, it is *your* fault; you are not articulating your points clearly and simply enough. You need to find a different approach, and yelling is not it. Calm down. Take a different approach. Ask what they don't understand. Perhaps ask them to explain what they think they understand so you can see the holes in their comprehension. Then clarify, reframe, expound, and continue talking them through the information until they understand it. Patience is appreciated and respected much more than a hot temper.

That being said, there are times when you might have to yell, but it should be extremely rare and calculated. I almost never yelled; the times I yelled in my twenty-year military career I can count on one hand. When I did, it left a mark. I only yelled because the situation required it, never because I lost my temper. I would yell to escalate and emphasize a message I was trying to get across to one of my guys, but only after he had failed to understand the seriousness after multiple attempts from me when I wasn't yelling.

Let's say one of my SEALs violated a rule. I wouldn't immediately jump down his throat. Instead, after the initial violation took place, I might start by saying, "Hey, you know you violated that rule. Were you aware of that?" He might explain why he had violated the rule, and usually that would be enough; he wouldn't violate it again. But if he did, I would have to escalate with something like, "This is the second time you violated this rule. You know that, right? Do you understand why we have this rule?" At that point, I would explain the rule to the wayward SEAL to make sure he understood not just what the rule was but why it was important not to violate it. Once I was done with this, and perhaps one more iteration of this type of escalation, I would seldom have another violation. Normally, I was able to get my people on the right track by providing a good explanation of what the rule was, exactly why it was important and how it impacted our strategic mission, and what the consequences of not following it were. Sometimes it might even take two or three conversations to get my point across.

But occasionally, I would get a SEAL for whom my words just weren't sinking in, and despite my multiple explanations, he would violate the rule again. I would escalate one level more and raise my voice to a yell. Again, this was an absolutely rare occurrence. When I did, I did it in private, I did it quickly, directly, and aggressively. There was no doubt about my emotion on the subject. *"You did this again, and it is absolutely unacceptable! I will not tolerate this again. Ever."* Then I would lower my voice into a controlled growl and say something like, "Am I making myself perfectly clear? And do you understand?"

At that point, the look on his face would be a combination of shock, fear, and, most important, understanding. Since it was the first time he had ever seen me yell, he instantly understood the seriousness of the situation. During my entire career, I never had to yell at someone twice.

That being said, yelling is seldom appropriate. Even if it was a calculated choice in your mind, you still give the impression that you have lost control if you are yelling. The other escalation would be writing someone up. After you have warned them multiple times, you may threaten them with writing them up and documenting their mistake. That can scare a lot of people straight. But if they violate a rule repeatedly, you do have to write them up—which should have an equivalent impact as yelling—and straighten them right out.

Of course, there are those people who do not change their behavior regardless of what you do to them. It is those people whose short-falls you as the leader must document, and, eventually, you must remove them from the team.

GETTING PEOPLE TO LISTEN

As you are rising through the ranks, you will need to have your say. When you speak, you will want people to listen. But sometimes, there will be people who do not listen, and they interrupt or talk over you. How should you handle that? The answer is fairly simple: let them talk. Let that person jump in and say what they want, and let them finish their thoughts. This works for a multitude of reasons.

If someone wants to talk a lot, then listen. There is no better cure for a person who wants to talk a lot than letting them get their thoughts out of their head. Let them say what they want to say. When they have nothing left, you will be able to make your point.

This is also good because as they unload all their ideas, you now know not only everything you know, you also know everything they know. Armed with this knowledge, you can assess their ideas. You can formulate counterpoints or recommendations around their thoughts. This works just as well, or even better, in a group where you listen to multiple people break down their own ideas, argue with one another, and ask questions of one another about details of their ideas. Once again, this whole time, you get to more clearly under-stand the thoughts of others while quietly strengthening your own thoughts or ideas around the subject. When you finally do find the opportunity to speak, you have the most comprehensive and developed thoughts.

The less you talk, the more people listen. Don't be the person who is always talking. Speak when you need to, but don't talk just to talk. You will find that when you listen to others speak and absorb what they say, you can formulate the most important and impactful statement of the discussion, which will increase your influence on the situation. Even if a debate among colleagues leaves you with nothing to add other than your approval, that well-articulated approval will carry more weight than blathering on just to hear yourself talk.

Don't waste your words. Let other people do that; instead, speak with poignancy and power.

APOLOGIZING

There are some leaders who think apologizing is a sign of weakness, but that is usually because they are weak and insecure about their leadership position.

There is nothing wrong with apologizing when you make a mistake. That is part of taking ownership. This is especially true in relationship situations where you have done something that had a negative impact on someone. You left them out, overlooked them, or otherwise disrespected them in some way. When that happens, apologies are completely acceptable; actually, an apology is more than acceptable, it is the right thing to do.

If you are apologizing because of a decision that was made, then the apology must also be accompanied by an explanation. Explain to the team why you did what you did: what you saw, how you read the situation, how you anticipated the decision would work out, what actually happened, and how you will prevent yourself from making the same mistake again. Then apologize for making the mistake—as long as you mean it. Don't apologize for every little slipup—not because it is bad to apologize but because it is bad to apologize if there is nothing really to apologize for. If there is no major negative result from the bad decision, then it likely doesn't warrant an actual apology. But if you feel you made an error and you feel you owe an apology, then give one.

If you find yourself in situations where you might not feel you owe an apology—you feel it wasn't your fault—first check your ego; chances are, there is something you could have done differently. Apologize for that. And if you truly think you weren't at fault, guess what? You are. And taking ownership is still an effective tool. Disarm the people who are looking to place blame by saying sorry and taking the blame yourself. Then find the solution and start moving toward it.

When I try to think of situations in which it is bad to apologize, I have a hard time doing it. I'm not scared to apologize. If I make a mistake, I am going to own it. If someone else makes a mistake and no one will own it, I will own that too. Perhaps that is why I so often found myself in leadership positions; I was willing to own things. I was willing to take the hit, to take the daggers from others. I was willing to apologize, own mistakes, and move forward. I recommend you do the same.

BE APPROACHABLE BUT CAREFUL WITH WORDS

It is easy for a chasm to develop between the leader and the troops, and that distance—caused by physical separation, a pay gap that results in a socioeconomic divide, or the rank structure in any organization—can become too much. To avoid this, make sure you close all these gaps to the best of your ability. Spend time with your people—go into the field with them, visit their offices, spend time at their jobsites. Don't flaunt your financial advantages by throwing money around or talking about how much you make or your ski vacation in Europe. And don't let your rank stifle good conversations. Speak with your troops not just about work but about life, family, and the future. Find out what you can about them. Know them. When a leader develops a good relationship with everyone in their chain of command, the gap is closed. The troops are more likely to discuss problems, share concerns, and divulge issues that might be brewing beneath the surface. This is critical for understanding the true climate and atmosphere within an organization.

But remember, even when you close that gap, there is still a line.

As a leader, you must be careful not to become too familiar, casual, and unguarded with the troops. Gossip, sarcasm, and flippant remarks all carry much too much weight when thrown around by a leader. Ribbing comments that might seem harmless among friends can have real impact on a subordinate. Even legitimate criticism needs to be delivered with caution, preferably in private, so that dignity is maintained. This is not to say that critical mistakes should not be reviewed so the whole team can learn, but criticism must be constructive and aimed not at an individual's potential but at the specific mistakes themselves.

A leader must choose their words very carefully and remember that their words can have immense impact; positive remarks can incite and intensify enthusiasm while negative remarks can fully crush spirits. So be judicious and thoughtful about what you say, who you say it to, and how you say it.

SET THE EXAMPLE

If you are in a leadership position, the team is watching you. Your people are watching your attitude. They are watching your behavior, and they don't miss a thing. If you are late for a meeting, they notice it. If you roll your eyes, they notice it. If you yawn, they are watching and are thinking you are tired or bored or both.

The team members are watching everything, and on top of that, they will imitate what they see. If you are late, they will be late too. If you dress like a slob, they will dress that same way. If you break the rules, they will also break the rules, so you have to behave correctly at all times. You have to be the ideal.

They will also, consciously or unconsciously, mimic your emotions. If you stay calm, so will they. If you panic, they will panic as well. If you have a negative attitude, their attitudes will also turn negative.

However, if you have a positive attitude, so will they. If you treat people with respect, remain humble, and act professionally, then your team, for the most part, will do the same.

What trips many leaders up is failing to understand how perceptive their subordinates are. Subordinates notice everything. They watch, they take notes, they discuss the leader's behavior among themselves. I know this because I was a subordinate. I was the youngest and most junior guy in my first two SEAL platoons. We were always watching our bosses.

Because your subordinates are watching so closely, it also means they will notice if you cover things up. If you make a mistake, don't try to cover it up. Admit it. Own it. Explain what you will do to prevent it from happening again. Don't lie to them; they will see right through it.

As a leader, you must remember you are being watched. And in everything you do, you must *set the example.*

CONCLUSION

IT IS ALL ON YOU, BUT NOT ABOUT YOU

When you are a leader, there are no excuses, and there is no one else
to blame. You have to make decisions. You have to build relationships. You have to communicate so that everyone can understand.
You have to control your ego and your emotions. You have to be
able to detach. You need to instill pride in the team. You need to
train the team. You need to be balanced and tactful and aware, and
you have to take ownership. The list goes on and on and makes up
this incredibly complex undertaking that we call *leadership.* And if
you do all those things well—if you lead effectively—the team will
be successful, and the mission will be accomplished. If you do not
lead effectively, you will fail, and the team will not accomplish the
mission.

Leadership is all on you.

But at the same time, leadership is not *about* you. Not at all. Leadership is about the team. The team is more important than you are.

The moment you put your own interests above the team and above the mission is the moment you fail as a leader. When you think you can get away with it—when you think the team won't notice your self-serving maneuvers—you are wrong. Your people will see it, and they will know it.

The leadership strategies and tactics in this book are to be used not so *you* can be successful; these strategies and tactics are to be used so *the team* can be successful. If you use them to further your own career or your own agenda, eventually, these strategies and tactics will backfire and bring you down. You will fail as a leader and as a person.

But if you use these strategies and tactics with the goal of helping others and of helping the team accomplish its mission, then the team will succeed. And if the team succeeds, you win as a leader and as a person. But infinitely more important, your people win. And that is true leadership.

INDEX